A2

English G 21

Klassenarbeitstrainer
für Schülerinnen und Schüler

mit Lösungen
Lerntipps
Kompetenztest

Vokabeltrainer-App

Verfügbar für: iOS, Android
und Windows Phone

W0030723

 Deine **Online-Angebote** findest du hier:

1. Melde dich auf scook.de an.
2. Gib den unten stehenden Zugangscode in die Box ein.
3. Hab viel Spaß mit den Online-Angeboten.

Dein Zugangscode auf
www.scook.de

Die Online-Angebote können dort
nach Bestätigung der AGB und
Lizenzbedingungen genutzt werden.

a2h4m-pjrgg

English G 21 • Band A 2

Klassenarbeitstrainer mit Lösungen und Lerntipps

Konzeption
Dr. Ursula Mulla und Nogi Mulla, Germering

Erarbeitet von
Bärbel Schweitzer M. A., Staufen

In Zusammenarbeit mit der Englischredaktion
Dr. Christiane Kallenbach (Projektleitung)
Stefanie Bayer (verantwortliche Redakteurin)
Susanne Bennetreu (Bildredaktion)

Beratende Mitwirkung
Angela Ringel-Eichinger, Bietigheim-Bissingen
Martina Schroeder, Stedtlingen
Bernd Sold, Bobenheim-Roxheim

Illustrationen
Constanze Schargan, Berlin
Roland Beier, Berlin (Lösungseinleger S. 30)

Bildquellen
Alamy, Abingdon (S. 8 boat: Michael Howard; S. 8 Oxford Street: PCL; S. 52 accident: Profimedia International s.r.o.);
Education Photos, Guilford (S. 21 fashion show: John Walmsley); Anthony Grimley, Bath (S. 39 fun run); Istock, Calgary
(S. 52 bike: David Morgan); Photolibrary, New York (S. 8 Buckingham Palace: Charles Bowman; S. 35, S. 38 boy: Hans Carlen);
Rob Cousins, Bristol (S. 83 kids in canteen, S. 46 hamster); Shutterstock, New York (S. 8 beach: Augustinho Goncalves; S. 17
Big Ben: Jenny Horne; S. 35, 41 dog: Eric Isselee; S. 35, 41 cat: Myth Photography; S. 35 elderly lady: Yuri Acurs; S. 35 young lady:
Factoria singular fotografia; S. 35 girl: Elene Elisseeva; S. 35 rabbit: Reddogs; S. 35 mouse: Ljupco Smokovski; S. 35 budgie:
Eric Isselee; S. 41 guinea pig: Sascha Burkard; S. 44 cat on sofa: Pavel Sazonov; S. 48 boy: Yuri Acurs; S. 48 girl with dark hair:
Konstantin Sutyagin; S. 48 girl with blond hair: Mityukhin Oleg Petrovich; S. 52 black car: Ben Smith; S. 52 white car: Vibrant
Image Studio; S. 65 man: Elene Elisseeva; S. 70 woman: Andresr; S. 70 teen girl: @erics; S. 70 man: Carsten Reisinger; S. 70 boy:
Galina Barskaya)

Titelbild
Constanze Schargan, Berlin; IFA-Bilderteam, Ottobrunn (Hintergrund Union Jack: Jon Arnold Images)

Layout und technische Umsetzung
Heike Freund, Hameln

Umschlaggestaltung
Klein & Halm Grafikdesign, Berlin

www.cornelsen.de
www.EnglishG.de

Soweit in diesem Lehrwerk Personen fotografisch abgebildet sind und ihnen von der Redaktion fiktive Namen, Berufe,
Dialoge und Ähnliches zugeordnet oder diese Personen in bestimmte Kontexte gesetzt werden, dienen diese Zuordnungen
und Darstellungen ausschließlich der Veranschaulichung und dem besseren Verständnis des Lehrwerksinhalts.

1. Auflage, 13. Druck 2017

Druck: H. Heenemann, Berlin

ISBN 978-3-06-031902-2

PEFC zertifiziert
Dieses Produkt stammt aus nachhaltig
bewirtschafteten Wäldern und kontrollierten
Quellen.
www.pefc.de
PEFC/04-31-1156

INHALT

ZUERST EIN PAAR BEMERKUNGEN …

Liebe Schülerin, lieber Schüler,

in diesem Klassenarbeitstrainer findest du zu jeder Unit zwei Klassenarbeiten, mit denen du alle Fertigkeiten (skills) trainieren kannst, die du für die Klassenarbeiten benötigst.

Das Üben für eine Klassenarbeit ist wie ein Puzzle: du brauchst mehrere Teile, die – zu einem Ganzen zusammengesetzt – deine optimale Vorbereitung sind.

Vorbereitung
Plane genügend Zeit ein. Mache einen Lernplan vor der Klassenarbeit. Hole dir bei Unklarheiten Hilfe. Am Tag vor der Arbeit wiederholst du nur kurz.

Lernheft
Besorge dir ein Schreibheft. Es dient für Schreibaufgaben und zusätzliche Übungen. Schreibe schön und übersichtlich (mit Überschrift, Aufgabe, Seite). Lege ein Inhaltsverzeichnis auf der 1. Seite an.

Lösungen
Du findest die Lösungen zusammen mit deinen Audios unter www.scook.de. Dort kannst du sie dir mit deinem Code freischalten. Dein Code steht am Anfang des Hefts auf der ersten Seite. Der Lösungsteil enthält die Lösungen, alle Hörtexte und viele nützliche Lerntipps und Lernpläne.

Wiederholung
Aufgaben, die dir noch schwer fallen, solltest du ein zweites oder drittes Mal machen.

Punkteschlüssel
Er hilft dir, deine Leistung einzuschätzen.

Listening Aufgaben
Lies Überschrift und Aufgaben in Ruhe durch. Höre den Text an. Bearbeite dann die Aufgaben. Höre den Text noch einmal an. Bearbeite die noch fehlenden Aufgaben.

Reading Aufgaben
Lies Überschrift und Text in Ruhe durch. Lies die Aufgaben, ohne sie zu bearbeiten. Lies den Text noch einmal. Markiere passende Stellen mit verschiedenen Farben! Bearbeite jetzt die Aufgaben.

Writing Aufgaben / Mediation Aufgaben
Lies die Aufgabe genau durch. Beachte Hilfestellungen in der Aufgabe. Notiere dir Stichworte. Schreibe deinen Text. Überprüfe ihn auf Vollständigkeit, Rechtschreibung und richtige Grammatik.

Speaking Aufgaben
Lies die Aufgabenstellung. Höre dir die Aufnahme online an. Sprich beim 2. Hören mit.

Wenn du regelmäßig übst, gewinnst du an Sicherheit bei der Bearbeitung der unterschiedlichen Aufgaben. Und: je besser du wirst, umso mehr Freude hast du beim Lernen und natürlich auch mit der englischen Sprache.

Übrigens: die Klassenarbeiten in diesem Heft prüfen das Gelernte sehr ausführlich ab. Du brauchst daher für die Bearbeitung länger als eine Schulstunde. Natürlich kannst du dir die Klassenarbeiten auch auf einzelne Tage aufteilen oder bestimmte Aufgaben ganz gezielt üben.

So, am besten, du fängst gleich an.

Ich wünsche dir viel Freude mit dem Klassenarbeitstrainer und ein erfolgreiches, gutes Schuljahr.

Have fun with English!

Bärbel Schweitzer

Gesamtpunktzahl mit Speaking	_____ / 65 Note _____
Gesamtpunktzahl ohne Speaking	_____ / 55 Note _____

LISTENING

_____ / 25

 01 **Paul's very special holiday**

You are listening to a radio programme. A reporter is interviewing Paul, a 13-year-old boy from Southampton.

☞ Lies im Vorwort, wie du **Listening**-Aufgaben gut lösen kannst.
Du kannst diese Aufgabe auch als **Reading**-Aufgabe machen.
Lies dazu den Hörtext in den **Lösungen** auf S. 2 und bearbeite dann die Aufgabe.

1   Where did Paul go?

_____ / 7

Look at the map (Landkarte) first. Then listen carefully. Put a cross (✘) in the countries where Paul went.

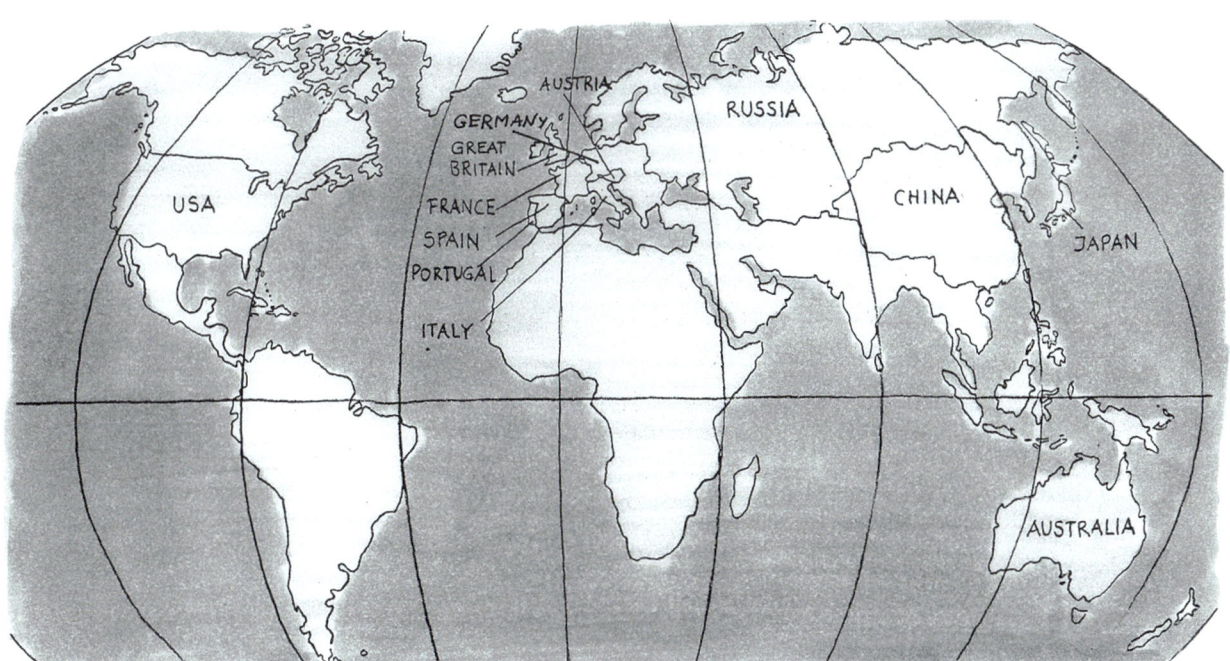

2   What was the weather like?

_____ / 8

Listen again, then tick (✔) the correct answer. Sometimes you must tick two boxes.

	warm	cold	sunny	rainy	hot	windy	stormy
Paris							
Berlin							
Munich *(München)*							
Rome *(Rom)*							
New York							
Miami							
Beijing *(Peking)*							
Sydney							

3   What do you know about Paul's holiday?

_____ / 10

Read the sentences first. Then listen to the CD again and tick (✔) the correct box.

		Right	Wrong
1	Paul went on holidays with his parents.		
2	Paul liked the museums in Berlin.		
3	Paul can speak French.		
4	Paul went to a museum in Munich.		
5	Paul wants to go to Munich again.		
6	The Italians were nice.		
7	Paul didn't like Miami.		
8	Paul was in China for one week.		
9	Paul's uncle lives in Shanghai.		
10	In Sydney it was wintertime and very cold.		

LANGUAGE

_____ / 20

1 WORDS Holiday words

_____ / 12

Find the words.

Spain is a _ _ _ _ _ _ _ .

There are three _ _ _ _ _ _ _ in the _ _ _ _ .

From up there you have a good _ _ _ _ _ .

Is the _ _ _ _ _ empty?

Yes, there is _ _ _ _ _ _ there.

Look, there is a little _ _ _ _ _ _ _

in the lake.

You live in a country and you go to another

country – you go _ _ _ _ _ _ _ _ .

Every August we stay in our

_ _ _ _ _ _ _ by the _ _ _ .

Can you make a word with the letters in the boxes ? Put them in the right order.

**t**

Mr and Mrs Miller always _ _ _ _ to Portugal.

2 WORDS Irregular simple past forms

_____ / 8

Fill in the infinitive, the irregular simple past form or the German translation.

Infinitive	Simple past form	German translation
		sich treffen
	shone	
		schwimmen
put		
	read	
		essen
ride		
throw		

WRITING

_____ / 10

A holiday postcard

Buckingham Palace   shopping in Oxford Street

You want to write a postcard to your friend Paul Wells in Edinburgh.
Choose one of the postcards and tell him:

– *where you are*
– *where you are staying*
– *what you did yesterday*
– *what you want to do today*
– *what the weather is like*
– *how long you are there*

*Write **6 or more** sentences and an ending into the postcard on p. 9.*

Dear Paul,

_____

_____

_____

_____

_____

_____

_____

_____

_____

Paul Wells

3, Arnhem Drive

Edinburgh EH2 2DG

SPEAKING

_____/10

🎧 02 **Talking about the holidays**

It's the first day at school after the holidays. The new teacher Mr Hall is talking to the class.
At the moment he is talking to Jenny. He is asking her questions about her holidays.

First listen to Mr Hall and Jenny.

🎧 03 **Now you**

Now Mr Hall is interviewing you.
Listen to his questions, then answer in complete sentences.
Halte den Text an, damit du Zeit für deine Antwort hast.

Use these notes for your answers:

- Ihr seid nach Italien gefahren.   (1)
- Ihr seid mit dem Auto gefahren.   (1)
- In der ersten Woche war das Wetter sehr warm und sonnig, an einem Tag sogar über
  dreißig Grad. In der zweiten Woche war es bewölkt, an einem Tag regnete es.   (2x 1,5)
- Ihr habt in eurem Wohnwagen gewohnt.   (1,5)
- Als das Wetter schlecht war, seid ihr in ein Museum gegangen. Sage auch, in welches
  Museum ihr gegangen seid, z. B. ins Spaghettimuseum.   (2,5)
- Ihr wart zwei Wochen weg.   (1)

Gesamtpunktzahl _____ / 65   Note _____

READING

_____ / 10

Bristol Times   *September 20*

Back to school

School started again last week. We asked our readers to tell us about their holidays. Here is one of the letters:

Well, holidays are sometimes difficult for the families: parents have to go to work but there is no school for the children. The problem is that many children watch television all day. So this year our children Ben (7) and David (12) went to Bristol Summer Camp. They were there from 10 o'clock in the morning to 5 o'clock in the afternoon from Monday to Friday.

They did lots of interesting things. Both Ben and David loved going to the summer camp from the first day. I can't think of a day when they didn't want to go.

Let me give you two examples of what they did. One day they worked on a "pirate ship", the next day they played on it and they read stories about pirates.
It was super for the kids!!!

Another day was "Radio Day". First they went to *Radio Bristol*, where they found out everything about the radio, and the next day they worked on their own radio programme. You could listen to it last Friday. It was great.

I can only say: the kids liked the summer camp and we, the parents, liked it, too!!!

Mrs Sue Lewis, Bristol

1   What did they do in the summer camp?

_____ / 4

Tick (✔) the two summer camp activities that Mrs Lewis wrote about.

2   Right – wrong?

_____/6

Tick (✔) the correct box.

		Right	Wrong
1	The holidays are over.	☐	☐
2	In the holidays Ben and David watched TV all day.	☐	☐
3	They were at the camp for 5 hours from Monday to Friday.	☐	☐
4	The children didn't want to go to the camp at first.	☐	☐
5	They went to a café called "The Pirate Ship".	☐	☐
6	The summer camp's radio programme was good.	☐	☐

LANGUAGE

_____/43

1   STUDY SKILLS Describing pictures

_____/14

Look at the picture and describe it. Use the words below for describing pictures and follow
the numbers to complete the sentences.

1   At the bottom of the picture there is the _____.

2   _____ there is a café.

3   _____ a family is sitting _____ the café.

4   _____ a young man _____.

5   _____ there are two girls. A young boy with a _____

is walking _____ them.

6   _____ there is an old _____.

7   _____ I can see a _____ in the _____.

> ☞ **Useful words:**
> on the left • on the right • at the top • at the bottom • in the middle •
> in the background • in the foreground • there is • there are
>
> **Tipp:**
> Um zu sagen, was gerade passiert, benutze das **present progressive**: Jo **is talking** to Jack.

2 WORDS Irregular verbs

_____/8

Fill in the missing forms of the irregular verbs.

Infinitive	Simple past form	German translation
	rode	
		holen, besorgen
teach		
		hören
	gave	
see		
	spoke	
		fliegen

3 GRAMMAR After the first week at the summer camp

_____/13

The first week at the summer camp is over. Ben and David tell their friends about the first week.
Complete what Ben and David said.
*Use the **simple past**. Be careful: sometimes you must use a negative form.*

> be (2x) • not/be • come • get up • go • have • play •
> read • not/read • not/stay • work • not/work

On Monday morning we _____ at 7.30 and _____ to the

camp for the first time. There _____ 40 boys and girls at the camp. Most of them

_____ from Bristol but some of them _____ from our school.

In the afternoon we _____ on the pirate ship. That _____ great.

On Tuesday we _____ on the ship. On Wednesday and Thursday we _____

stories about pirates. After that we _____ on our ship and _____ a

really good time. We _____ comics and we _____ in bed all day long.

 Bei dieser Übung und der nächsten geht es um das **simple past**. Du sollst **bejahte Aussage-sätze** (positive statements) und **verneinte Aussagesätze** (negative statements) bilden. Lies dazu noch einmal die **Grammar Files** 1 und 2 in deinem Englischbuch auf S. 127/128.

4   GRAMMAR What Ben and David did and what they didn't do

_____ / 8

Here are some pictures of what the two brothers did at the summer camp and what they didn't do.
*Write positive and negative statements in the **simple past**.*

1 _____   2 _____

3 _____   4 _____

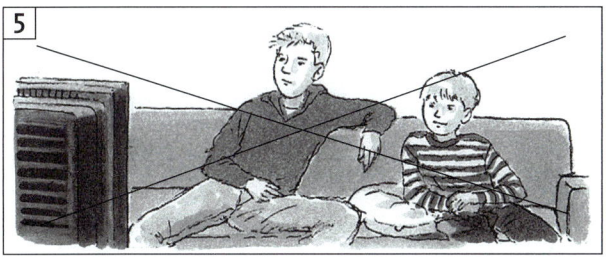   

5 _____   6 _____

7 _____   8 _____

☞ **Simple past positive statements**
Regelmäßige Verben: stay ▶ stay**ed**
Unregelmäßige Verben: meet ▶ **met** (2. Form)

Simple past negative statements
didn't + Infinitiv: he **didn't stay**, she **didn't meet**

MEDIATION

_____ / 12

David helps his brother Ben

At Bristol Summer Camp there are lots of boys and girls. Ben likes playing with Florian, a seven-year-old boy from Germany. Florian doesn't speak much English and Ben doesn't speak any German. So David helps them. Complete the dialogue.

Ben   It's nice that you are here in our summer camp, Florian. Are you on holiday here in Bristol?

David   Ben sagt, dass es schön ist, dass du _____

             _____

Florian Ja, ich bin für zwei Wochen hier. Ich wohne im Haus meiner Tante hier in Bristol.

David   He says that he is here _____. He is _____

             _____

Ben   And where does his aunt live?

David   Und wo _____

Florian Sie wohnt hinter der Kirche in der Cumberland Street Nummer 7.

David   She _____

Ben   Well, that's great. We only live a mile away. We can come here together in the mornings.
             We always go by bike.

David   _____

             _____

             _____

Florian Ja, das ist eine gute Idee. Wir können auch heute gleich nach dem Summer Camp zusammen
             nach Hause gehen.

David   He likes the idea. He says we can _____.

             _____

Ben   Yes, we can. But now we must help with the lunch. Let's go.

Klassenarbeit B

Gesamtpunktzahl ohne Speaking _____ / 70 Note _____
Gesamtpunktzahl mit Speaking _____ / 85 Note _____

LISTENING

_____ / 13

🎧 04 **Bristol today**

👉 Du kannst diese Aufgabe auch als **Reading**-Aufgabe machen.
Du findest den Text auf S. 9 in den **Lösungen**.

1 At the summer camps

_____ / 5

Listen to the radio programme "Bristol Today". Find out how long the children stayed at which summer camp. Tick (✔) the correct box.

	How long?			Which summer camp?				
	1 week	2 weeks	3 weeks	football camp	Bristol Summer Camp	riding camp	circus[1] camp	music camp
Sarah	☐	☐	☐	☐	☐	☐	☐	☐
Peter	☐	☐	☐	☐	☐	☐	☐	☐
Jason	☐	☐	☐	☐	☐	☐	☐	☐
Simon	☐	☐	☐	☐	☐	☐	☐	☐
David	☐	☐	☐	☐	☐	☐	☐	☐

[1] circus ['sɜːkəs]   *Zirkus*

2 The children and their holidays

_____/ 8

*Listen again and find the **eight correct** statements. Please tick (✔) them.*

Sarah	a) was at a camp in Scotland for two weeks.	☐
	b) went horse riding in the afternoons.	☐
	c) cleaned the horses in the mornings and in the afternoons.	☐
	d) thinks that one week is not long enough.	☐
Peter	a) went to a circus one day.	☐
	b) learned everything about dogs.	☐
	c) showed his parents what he learned at the camp.	☐
	d) says that his families and friends didn't like the camp.	☐
Jason	a) played football with boys and girls all day long.	☐
	b) practised hard and learned many things.	☐
	c) says that three weeks is too long.	☐
	d) wants to go to a football camp again.	☐
Simon	a) says that his camp was in a school.	☐
	b) didn't like the rooms.	☐
	c) says that there were boys and girls from all parts of Britain at his camp.	☐
	d) and the other boys and girls played in a musical.	☐
David	a) stayed at the camp day and night.	☐
	b) only went to the camp in the afternoons.	☐
	c) did lots of interesting activities.	☐
	d) rode his bike.	☐

LANGUAGE

_____/ 37

1 GRAMMAR Lunch break at school

_____/ 5

The boys and girls of Cotham School are talking about their holidays.
*Complete the dialogue with **was/wasn't/were/weren't**.*

David   My brother and I _____ at Bristol

Summer Camp. It _____ great.

What about you, where _____ you?

Susan   My parents and I _____ in Spain.

It _____ hot and sunny. We _____ there for long, only for 10 days.

Jeremy   So, the weather _____ good in Spain. I _____ in Ireland.

It _____ hot and sunny there, it _____ very wet and windy.

Simple past von **(to) be**
Beim **simple past** von **(to) be** gibt es nur zwei Formen:
I, he, she, it　　**was**
you, we, they　**were**

2　GRAMMAR　About the weekend

_____ / 6

It's Monday and Sally is asking Charlie about his weekend.
Complete Sally's questions with the correct question word.

 Question words
　　where, what, who, when, why

1　*Sally*　　_____ did you go at the weekend, Charlie?

　　Charlie　I was in London.

2　*Sally*　　_____ did you go with?

　　Charlie　I went with my aunt and uncle from Oxford.

3　*Sally*　　_____ did you stay in London?

　　Charlie　We stayed at a big hotel outside London.

4　*Sally*　　_____ did you stay outside London?

　　Charlie　Because it was not so expensive.

5　*Sally*　　_____ did you come back home from London?

　　Charlie　At 8 o'clock on Sunday evening.

6　*Sally*　　And ..., _____ do you think about London?

　　Charlie　Well, what a question, it was just great, great, great!!!

3   GRAMMAR An interview

_____ / 14

George is at Southend Comprehensive School. Today he wants to interview his form teacher Mr Wilson for the school magazine. Write down his questions for the interview on the note pad.

George wants to ask his form teacher

1. about his **past**
   - when – come to this school
   - why – want to be a teacher
   - – go to school in Bristol
   - where – stay in your last holidays

2. about his life as a teacher **today**
   - what – teach
   - – like your job
   - when – get up in the morning
   - what – do in your free time

Notes for the interview

Past:

When did you come to this school?

_____

_____

_____

Today:

_____

_____

_____

_____

☞ Beachte bei dieser Übung, dass du sowohl Fragen im **simple present** (today) als auch im **simple past** (past) bilden sollst.

Fragen mit **do/does – simple present**	**Fragen** mit **did – simple past**
1 ohne Fragewort ▶ **Do** you sing?	1 ohne Fragewort ▶ **Did** you sing?
2 mit Fragewort ▶ **What do** you sing?	2 mit Fragewort ▶ **What did** you sing?

4   WORDS Irregular verbs

_____ / 8

Find eight irregular verbs and write the infinitive, the simple past form and the German translation of the infinitive.

Infinitive	Simple past form	German translation
1 h *ear*	_____	_____
2 t _____	_____	_____
3 d _____	_____	_____
4 k _____	_____	_____
5 m _____	_____	_____
6 r _____	_____	_____
7 s _____	_____	_____
8 e _____	_____	_____

5   WORDS   Say it in English

_____ / 4

Was sagst du, wenn du ...

1   zu jemandem sagen willst, er oder sie solle sich um seine/ihre eigenen Angelegenheiten kümmern?

_____ .

2   zu jemandem sagen willst, dass etwas überhaupt nicht in Frage kommt?

_____ .

3   zu jemandem sagen willst: „Na, hör mal!"?

_____ .

4   jemanden fragen willst, ob er/sie das wirklich glaubt?

_____ .

WRITING

_____ / 20

An e-mail to Germany

Simon is an English boy from Bristol. In his holidays he was in Scotland at an international music camp. He met Kai, a boy from Munich, Germany. At the end of September he writes an e-mail to Kai.

Er schreibt,

- wann er wieder mit der Schule begann und was es Neues aus der Schule gibt,
- dass er das *international music camp* super fand,
- dass er viel gelernt hat,
- dass er hofft, mal wieder in ein *music camp* gehen zu können.

Er fragt Kai,

- ob es Kai im *music camp* auch gefallen hat,
- ob er wieder mal nach Großbritannien kommen möchte,
- ob er auch viel Englisch in Schottland gelernt hat,
- was er in den letzten zwei Wochen seiner Ferien gemacht hat.

Er bittet Kai,

- ihm etwas aus der deutschen Schule zu erzählen.

Beginne und beende deine E-Mail.
Schreibe den Text der E-Mail in dein Lernheft.

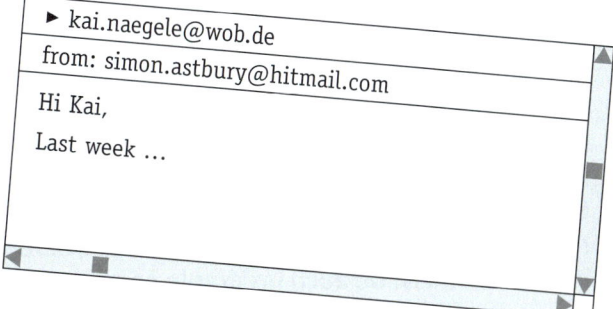

► kai.naegele@wob.de
from: simon.astbury@hitmail.com
Hi Kai,
Last week ...

SPEAKING

/ 15

🎧 05 **Last Sunday**

Sarah, Susan, Tim and David are talking about last Sunday. Listen to Sarah.

Now you

*Now you take David's part. Look at the ideas in the box. Choose some of them or think of new ideas. Take notes about David's Sunday from morning to night in the calendar. Write down **ten notes**.*

Ideas:
help my mother/father/brother • play basketball • read books • meet my friends • do my homework • watch TV • have breakfast with ... • have lunch • have tea • go to my friend/ grandma • go to a museum ... • play football • talk on the phone to ... • tidy my room

4 October		**Sunday**
8.00	*got up ...*	
9.00	*had breakfast with ...*	
10.00		
11.00		
12.00		
13.00		
14.00		
15.00		
16.00		
17.00		
18.00		
19.00		
20.00		
21.00		

☞ ▪ Höre dir Sarahs Ausführungen nochmal genau an. Schreibe dir alle **Zeitangaben** (time phrases) und alle **Bindewörter** (linking words) heraus. Du findest den Text auch auf S. 12 in den **Lösungen**.
▪ Baue sie in deine Ausführungen ein. Benutze unterschiedliche Satzanfänge, z.B. in the morning, after breakfast, at 11 o'clock, then, before, ...
▪ Wie Sarah musst du auch im **simple past** sprechen.

Now tell Sarah, Susan and Tim about last Sunday. You are David. Say about ten sentences.

Gesamtpunktzahl _____ / 85   Note _____

READING

____ / 22

Last month Becca Green wrote an article for the school magazine.

This year's fashion show – a hit

by Becca Green, Form 9 TG

Our school always has a fashion show in October. This year it was really fantastic. Forms 8, 9 and 10 invited the other students, the teachers and all the parents and grandparents. The assembly hall[1] was more than full – there were about 600 people. Everybody wanted to see this year's ideas. The 'models' were nervous, but our presenter Luke Smith from Form 10AR was even more nervous.

He was the most nervous person of all! But after the first two minutes he relaxed and was the best presenter ever. He explained the different parts of the show and was funny at the same time.

The forms thought of the most interesting topics for the fashion show. Form 8 HG showed wonderful clothes from India, and did an Indian dance. The girls looked so beautiful. Form 9 TG made hats from different materials: newspapers, paper bags, old CDs. You could see big and small hats, funny and elegant hats. Their 'school hats' were really a highlight. They designed ten special hats for our school uniform. It was only a joke but everybody liked the idea. Form 10 FR's topic was 'new attics' and they showed fashions from the 1980s. Presenter Luke explained that most of these clothes were over 20 years old and came from their parents' attics. The grandparents had fun when they saw their children's old dresses, trousers, T-shirts and blouses again!

Another good thing was that the forms had great music for the show. Form 8 HG had slow and quiet Indian music, 9 TG sang songs about hats in their presentation and 10 FR had CDs from the 1980s. The parents and grandparents sang to the music, and even some of the teachers sang too!

Well, this year's fashion show was a hit. Thank you to all the boys and girls of the organisation team.

[1] assembly hall [ə'semblı hɔːl] *Aula*

1 The fashion show

_____/ 12

Fill in the mind map with information from the text.

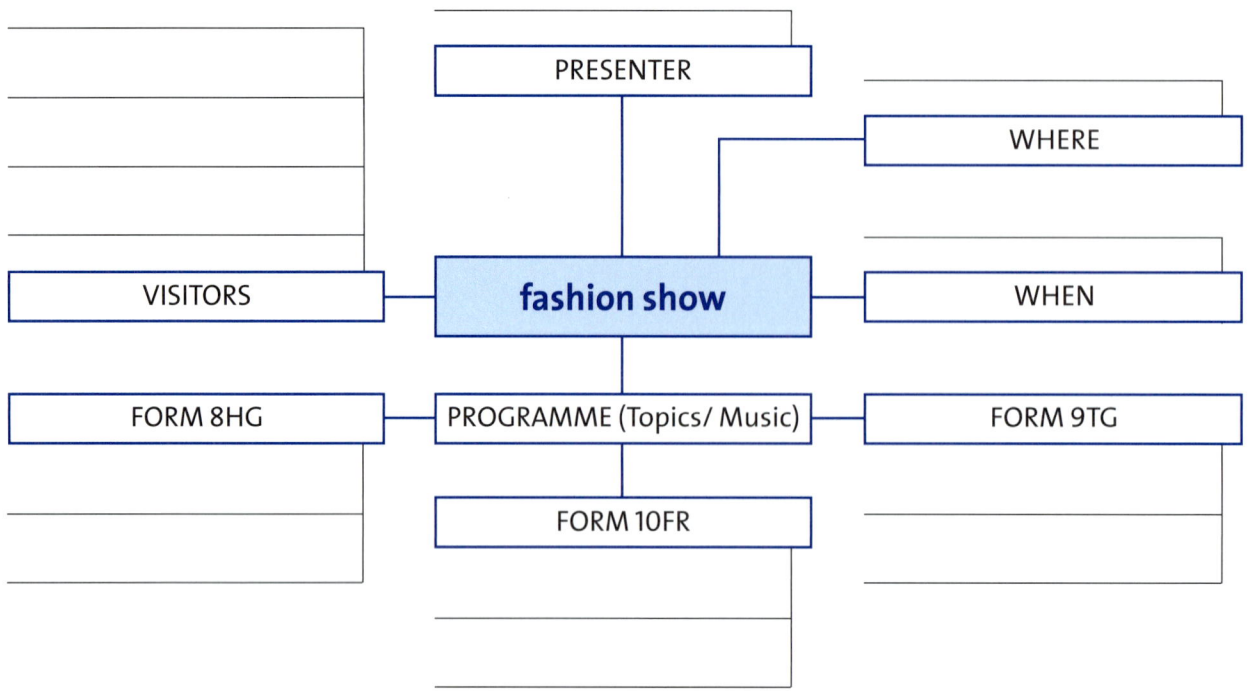

2 More about the fashion show

_____/ 10

Put 17 ticks (✔) in the correct boxes.

☞ In jeder Zeile findest du die Angabe in Klammern, wie viele Häkchen du machen musst.

The school	The models	Luke Smith	The show	Form 8 HG	Form 9 TG	Form 10 FR	The parents	The grandparents	The teachers	
										had music from a CD. (2)
										was one of the best shows in the last years. (1)
										explained why the name for the fashion of Form 10 FR was 'new attics'. (1)
										sang while the models presented. (4)
										presented old-fashioned clothes. (1)
										has a fashion show every year. (1)
										was/were very nervous. (2)
										had a topic for their show. (3)
										presented fashion from another country. (1)
										showed hats from recycled material. (1)

LANGUAGE

_____ / 54

1 WORDS What people said after the fashion show

_____ / 7

Fill in the correct words. Be careful – there are two words in the box that you don't need.

> spend time on • love • recycling • presenter •
> even • more than • join • everybody • cheap

Betty   I _____ fashion shows – they're fantastic. Luke was our _____.

He was great.

Susan   There were _____ 600 people in the assembly hall!

_____ liked the fashion show!

Mr Hall   Why didn't you _____ me, Susan? The show was super.

John   I thought, oh no, not again. I didn't want to _____ another boring fashion show.

But this one was different.

Form teacher Great idea, form 9TG – you used old stuff for new hats. A great example of _____.

2 WORDS Clothes

_____ / 12

*Fill in the chart with words that have to do with clothes. Find **four** words or more each.*

Clothes		
What you can wear: (nouns)	What you can do with them: (verbs)	How you can describe them: (adjectives)
1 hat	1 buy	1 warm
2	2	2
3	3	3
4	4	4
5	5	5

3   GRAMMAR This year's fashion show

_____ / 7

Here is what Joe said about the fashion show. Complete the sentences with the right forms of the adjectives.

The fashion show was super!! The colours of the Indian clothes were _____

(beautiful) than the others. The music of form 8 HG was _____ (quiet) than

the music of the other forms. The hats of 9 TG were _____ (cheap) than the

clothes of 8 HG and 10 FR. I think our school uniform can look _____

(funny) with one of the hats. But with a hat it is _____ (expensive) than at the

moment. There were _____ (many) topics than the years before. This year's

fashion show was _____ (good) than last year's show.

4   GRAMMAR What do you think?

_____ / 3

Write complete sentences and choose adjectives from the box.

> nice • interesting • boring • difficult • exciting

Example: football match – fashion show

I think a football match is more interesting than a fashion show.

1 skirt – trousers

   _____

2 English – Maths

   _____

3 computer games – TV

   _____

> ☞ **a) Comparison with -er/est:** Einsilbige Adjektive/Adjektive auf -y
>   young – younger – youngest
>   lat**e** – later – latest
>   hot – ho**tt**er – ho**tt**est
>   pre**tty** – pre**tti**er – pre**tti**est
>
>   **b) Comparison with more/most:** Andere zwei- und mehrsilbige Adjektive
>   boring – more boring – most boring
>   difficult – more difficult – most difficult
>
>   **c) Irregular comparison:**
>   good – better – best
>   bad – worse – worst
>   much/many – more – most

5 GRAMMAR Making a hat for the fashion show   ____ / 5

Claire's mum helps her with her hat for the fashion show. Complete their dialogue with:

> some (2x) • any • something • anything

    some und die mit **some** zusammengesetzten Wörter stehen vor allem in **bejahten Sätzen**
any und die mit **any** zusammengesetzten Wörter stehen vor allem in **verneinten Sätzen** und **Fragen**

Claire   Mum, I need _____ help with my hat for the fashion show.

I haven't got _____ good ideas.

Mum   I think we can find _____ nice for your hat in the box up in the attic.

Claire   Oh, yes, let's go up there. Look, there are _____ funny paper bags.

I think I can use them.

Mum   Do you need _____ else?

Claire   Well, I need …

6 GRAMMAR Before the fashion show   ____ / 8

Lucy and Claire from 9 TG are talking about the fashion show.
Complete the sentences with the following possessive pronouns:

> yours • mine • theirs • ours • hers

Lucy   Our show is a big surprise. What about the students of form 10 FR?

Do you know anything about _____?

Claire   No, I don't. But I know that _____ is great. Our hats are a super idea.

My mum helped me with my hat, so _____ is ready.

What about _____, Lucy? Is your hat ready?

Lucy   Well, _____ is almost ready. Did you see Jenny's hat? _____ is super.

Can I see _____ now, Claire?

Claire   So what do you think of my hat, Lucy?

Lucy   Wow, _____ is the best, really!

    Um das richtige Possessivpronomen herauszufinden, solltest du dir zunächst überlegen, welches Nomen ersetzt werden soll.
Wähle dann das passende Pronomen aus.

Beispiel:
My birthday party was super. What about you? How was (**your birthday party** ▶) **yours**?

7 GRAMMAR What are they going to do?

_____/8

Look at the team plan for the fashion show. Sometimes they have changed[1] their plan.
So write what everybody is or is not going to do

1 Year 8 isn't _____.

2 They _____.

3 Year 9 _____.

4 Year 10 _____.

5 They _____.

6 Year 9 and Year 10 _____.

7 They _____.

8 Year 8 and Year 9 _____.

8 GRAMMAR Their teachers want to help: What are you going to do?

_____/4

The form teachers want to help the students with their fashion show.
So they are asking them a lot of questions. Write their questions with the correct form of the verbs.

1 What clothes _____ (wear)?

2 When _____ (present) the fashion show?

3 Who _____ (be) the presenter?

4 How _____ (get) the money for the fashion show?

 Im **Grammar File 7** im Englischbuch auf S. 131 kannst du nachschlagen, wie man das **going to-future** bildet.

---

[1] (to) change [tʃeɪndʒ] *ändern*

MEDIATION

_____/ 10

Preparing the show

The students of Cotham School are preparing the fashion show.
Jessica, a German girl, is an exchange student[1] at Cotham school at the moment.
Her English is not so good. She wants some information about the show and talks to Lucy in form 9 TG.
You are an English student at Cotham School and help Jessica.

Jessica Was geschieht hier?

You Jessica wants to know what is happening here.

Lucy We're preparing our fashion show.

You Lucy sagt, _____.

Jessica Frag sie bitte, wer die Modenschau präsentiert.

You Jessica wants to know who _____.

Lucy Every year the boys and girls of the forms 8, 9 and 10 present it.

You Sie sagt, _____.

Jessica Ist eine Modenschau jedes Jahr nicht langweilig?

You She wants to know if (ob) a fashion show _____.

Lucy Sometimes yes. But this year every form has a different topic, so it can't be boring.

You _____.

Jessica Und wann ist die Modenschau? Ich möchte gerne kommen.

You _____.

Lucy Great. It's on Saturday evening.

You _____.

[1] exchange student [ɪks'tʃeɪndʒ ˌstjuːdnt]   *Austauschschüler/in*

| Gesamtpunktzahl ohne Speaking | _____ / 70 Note _____ |
| Gesamtpunktzahl mit Speaking | _____ / 80 Note _____ |

LISTENING

_____ / 14

🎧 06 **Presentation of a project**

The students of form 7 DH are presenting their project 'Our school garden'. Listen to Mike, Sally and Carol.

> **New words**
> head teacher [ˌhed 'tiːtʃə] *Schulleiter/in;* flower ['flaʊə] *Blume;* bench [bentʃ] *(Sitz-)Bank;* expert ['ekspɜ] *Experte/Expertin;* plant [plɑːnt] *Pflanze*

1 **The project**

_____ / 8

What did they do in their project? Look at the pictures and put them in the right order:

2   HEADS AND TAILS About the school garden   ____ / 6

Listen again and match the heads and tails of these sentences. Draw lines.
There are two more endings than you need.

a) they worked together with other classes.

1   Form 7 DH

2   The students and Mrs Wallace

3   When the head teacher agreed

b) bought cakes in the school breaks.

c) everybody looked at the new school garden.

d) presented their project to their parents.

4   The form needed help

5   The other students of the school

6   With the money from the cakes

7   At the end of the presentation

e) talked about the project together.

f) so they asked somebody from the flower shop.

g) they bought plants and flowers.

h) had lots of problems together.

i) they started with the school garden.

LANGUAGE   ____ / 41

1   GRAMMAR Questions about the project   ____ / 6

The guests in the new school garden ask a lot of questions about the project.
*Complete their questions with **How much / How many**.*

1   _____ time did you have for the project?

2   _____ parents helped you with the project?

3   _____ money did you need for the plants?

4   _____ cakes did you make?

5   _____ sugar[1] did you need for all the cakes?

6   _____ students worked in the presentation group?

2   WORDS Say it in English   ____ / 6

1   Was ist los?   _____

2   Wem gehören diese CDs? *(Wessen CDs sind das?)* _____

3   Ich stimme dir zu.   _____

4   Was ist dein Standpunkt?   _____

5   Was machst du gerade?   _____

6   Mach kein Durcheinander.   _____

[1] sugar [sʊɡə]   *Zucker*

3 WORDS Opposites

_____ / 12

1 cheap ◄► _____

2 better ◄► _____

3 right ◄► _____

4 fantastic ◄► _____

5 (to) finish ◄► _____

6 boring ◄► _____

7 fast ◄► _____

8 (to) save money ◄► _____

9 (to) find ◄► _____

10 smaller ◄► _____

11 (to) take clothes off ◄► _____

12 (to) love ◄► _____

4 GRAMMAR What they can buy

_____ / 8

The students of 7 DH talk about their garden project and what they want to buy for their garden.
Look at the pictures and make comparisons. Write two sentences for each picture.

Example:

The apple cake is sweeter than the chocolate cake. The cheese cake is the sweetest.

sweet

beautiful

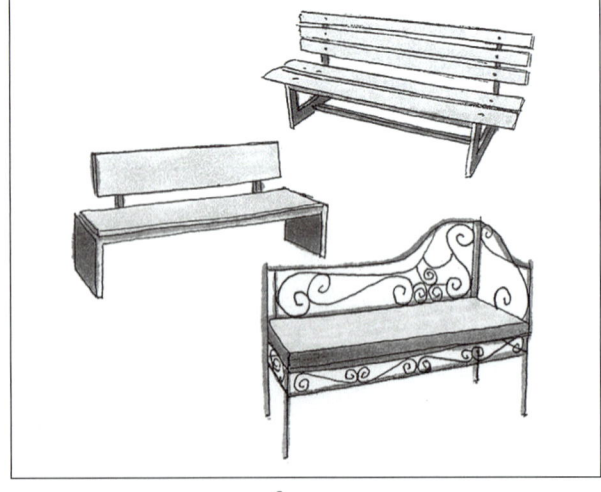

funny

The second bench is ...

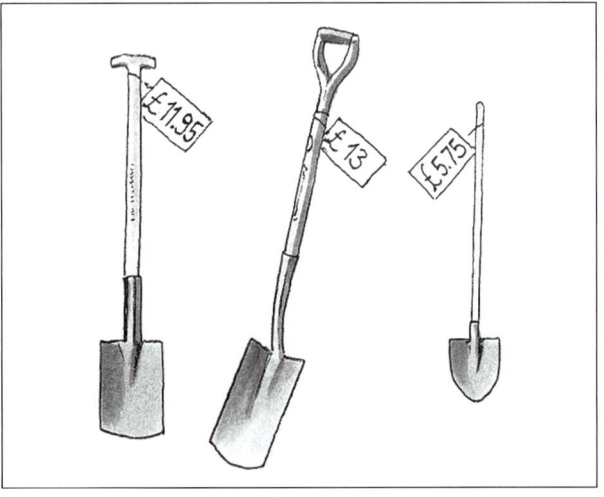

cheap

The first spade ...

5   GRAMMAR About yourself

_____/4

Tell us about yourself and compare yourself to some people who you know.
*Use **4 different adjectives** and **4 different structures** (siehe Hinweishand).*

1   I'm *older than* my friend.

2   In my class I'm the _____ student.

3   I'm _____ my aunt/uncle.

4   I'm _____ my teacher.

5   I'm _____ my cousin/brother/sister.

> **Comparison**
> ▶ Sue is **as** old **as** Tim.
> ▶ Tom is older **than** Jeremy.
> ▶ Jeremy is **not as** old **as** Tom.
> ▶ Tom is **the** oldest.

6   GRAMMAR Working in the school garden

_____/5

The kids are working in the garden.
Complete their dialogue with:

> somewhere • anywhere • somebody • anybody (2x)

Mike   Can _____ help me with the flowers here? Where can we put them?

Sally   We should put them _____ sunny.

Carol   You're right. Well, I'm looking for the spade. I can't find it _____ .

Can _____ see it?

Mike   I think _____ put it behind the tree. Just check there.

> **some** und die mit some zusammengesetzten Wörter stehen vor allem in **bejahten Sätzen**
> **any** und die mit any zusammengesetzten Wörter stehen vor allem in **verneinten Sätzen** und **Fragen**

WRITING

_____ / 15

An article for the school magazine

You are writing an article for the school magazine about the school garden project.
*Use the following key words and write at least **eight** complete sentences.*

1 topic – school garden

2 old garden – not nice

3 but! – no money

4 make and sell cakes – school – Bristol Market

5 need help – Mr Hull from the flower shop – parents

6 end of the project – presentation – parents

7 cakes and drink – say thank you

You can start like this:

The school garden

I'm writing about our school project. Our topic was …

_____

_____

_____

_____

_____

_____

_____

_____

_____

Verwende das **simple past** (sell ▶ sold).
Achte auf die **Satzstellung S – V – O**:

In the afternoon we played football.

SPEAKING

_____ / 10

🎧 07 **Two countries – two projects**

Sally is one of the students of 7 DH who did the school garden project. She tells you about the project and asks you questions about a project at your school. Listen to her and answer her questions.

☞ Höre dir Sallys Ausführungen und Fragen zuerst einmal an.
Überlege dir anhand der Zeichnungen, wie du ihre Fragen beantworten kannst.
Mache Notizen in die Tabelle auf S. 34.
Höre dir dann den Text ein 2. Mal an und beantworte Sallys Fragen.
Halte den Text an, damit du Zeit für deine Antworten hast.

awful classroom – old lamps

paint classroom – put up new lamps

who could help? – get money from

flea market[1] – old books

one Saturday – parents and students – paint –
put up new lamps – classroom

presentation – parents and teachers

[1] flea market ['fli: ˌmɑːkɪt]   _Flohmarkt_

Sally's questions	Your ideas
What was your project about?	
Tell me why you started the project.	
What about your form, did you have any problems too?	
How did you get the money for the project?	
How did you go on with your project and who helped you?	
What about your presentation?	

Two countries – two projects

Sally Hi! I'm Sally, I'm from Bristol. I want to tell you something about our school garden project.

What about you? What was your project about?

You Our project was …

Sally That's interesting. Let me tell you why we started our project.

You see, we had this old school garden at our school. It looked awful.

So one day we had the idea to make it nicer. But now tell me why you started your project.

You …

Sally Good idea. Now, we really had a problem because we needed an expert and we needed

money for the plants. What about your form, did you have any problems, too?

You …

Sally We sold cakes at school and at the market in Bristol. How did you get the money for the project?

You …

Sally Good! When we had the money, we started working in the garden. It looks super now, really.

How did you go on with your project and who helped you?

You …

Sally At the end we presented the project to our parents and the teachers. What about your presentation?

You …

LISTENING

Gesamtpunktzahl _____ / 55   Note _____

_____ / 16

 08 **Pets in Bristol**

Listen to a radio programme. Today people can call and talk about their pets.

☞ Lies in deinem Englischbuch das **Skills File** zu **Listening** auf S. 119 durch.
Wenn du einen Signalton hörst, kannst du den Text stoppen, um die
Fragen in Aufgabe 1 und 2 zu beantworten.

1 Pets and people

_____ / 8

Look at the photos and draw lines from the persons to the pet that they are talking about.
Then draw lines to the pets' names. Be careful: there are two more pets and four more pets' names than you need.

Mrs Hall

(2x)

 Pizza

??

Mr Benson

Mary

Mousy

Mickey

Mrs Gray

Noodle

Josh

Mr Bean

Polly

2   About the radio programme

_____ / 8

*Listen again. Tick (✔) the **eight correct** answers. There can be more than one correct answer.*

> ☞   Lies in deinem Englischbuch das **Skills File** zu **Multiple-choice exercises** auf S. 118 durch.

In today's radio programme	a) the presenter asks questions about the callers' pets.	☐
	b) people can talk to the presenter.	☐
	c) only people with problems can call.	☐
Mrs Hall	a) liked going for a walk with her pet.	☐
	b) will be OK again next week.	☐
	c) has got a problem with her neighbour.	☐
Mary	a) always cleans the pet's cage.	☐
	b) sometimes helps her mum.	☐
	c) still goes to school.	☐
Mrs Gray	a) has got a problem with her pet.	☐
	b) and her neighbours have got a pet together.	☐
	c) is at home all day.	☐
Josh	a) has got a pet.	☐
	b) can't have a pet.	☐
	c) will get Mrs Hall's telephone number.	☐

LANGUAGE

_____ / 28

1   WORDS Find the words.

_____ / 9

Find the words and fill them in.

1   You can watch it on TV every week: ☐ __ ☐ __ __ __ .

2   You put rubbish in a __ __ __ ☐ __ __ __ .

3   When you want to go on holiday and you have got a pet it's __ __ __ __ __ __ ☐ __ __

     that somebody looks after your pet.

4   The opposite[1] of happy is __ __ __ .

5   The opposite of friend is ☐ __ __ __ __ .

6   If you are __ __ __ you can't go to school.

7   If you are cold in bed you can put a ☐ __ __ – ☐ __ __ __ __ __ __ __ __ __ ☐ into your bed.

     It will keep you warm.

8   If you __ __ __ __ __ __ ☐ to do something you will do it and you must do it.

9   If you like somebody very much you can call him or her your ☐ ☐ ☐ ☐ t ☐ ☐ ☐ ☐ ☐ .

(You can make the word with the letters from the boxes if you put them in the right order.)

[1] opposite ['ɒpəzɪt]   *Gegenteil*

2 WORDS Who is at the animal party?

_____/8

Count the animals and write down who came to the party.

1 There are three _____.   6 There _____ two _____.

2 There is one _____.   7 _____

3 There are two _____.   8 _____

4 There are three _____.   9 _____

5 There _____ one _____.   10 _____

> ☞ Wiederholung von **there is / there are**:
> Du verwendest **there is** ..., wenn eine Angabe in der **Einzahl** folgt. (There **is one** lion.)
> Du verwendest **there are** ..., wenn eine Angabe in der **Mehrzahl** folgt. (There **are three** foxes.)

3 GRAMMAR What will life be like in 20 years?

_____/5

Write sentences about life in 20 years.

Example:

people – not read – many books: In twenty years people won't read many books.

1 people – have – fast and safe cars

_____

2 students – not have – teachers – have – computers only (2p)

_____

3 there – be – no more shops in small villages

_____

4 people – buy – everything – on the internet

_____

> ☞ Um auszudrücken, was in der Zukunft geschehen wird, benutzt du **will + Infinitiv**.
> Es gibt für **alle** Personen nur **eine Form**: I/you/he/she/it/they will ...
> Die Kurzform von will ist **'ll**: I'll, you'll usw.

4 GRAMMAR What Josh will do if he gets a dog:

_____ / 6

Finish Josh's sentences.

1 If my parents buy a dog for me, I …

2 I'll call her Lulu if …

3 If the weather is nice, …

4 I'll take Lulu to the animal clinic if …

5 I'll help in the kitchen if …

6 If my friends come to my house, …

1 _____

2 _____

3 _____

4 _____

5 _____

6 _____

☞ **Bedingungssätze Typ 1 (Conditional sentences type 1)**
Die Bedingung steht im if-Satz, die Folge für die Zukunft davon steht im Hauptsatz.

if – Satz (Bedingung)	Hauptsatz (Folge für die Zukunft)
simple present	*future oder can, must oder ein Imperativ*
If you **give** a hedgehog water,	it'**ll be** happy.
If you **go** to Bristol Zoo,	you **can watch** many different animals.
If Jack **does** his homework	he **can play** football longer.

WRITING

/ 11

A letter to Ian

You and your friends went to a fun run last week.
Write a letter to your friend Ian in Glasgow and tell him about the fun run. Use the flyer below.

Write

– why you think a fun run is a good idea (2P)

– who or what the fun run was for (1P)

– about your sponsor: Who was it? How did you find him/her?
  How much money did he/she give you for each mile? (3P)

– who you ran with (1P)

– how many miles you ran together (1P)

– what you liked best (2P)

– an end (1P)

You can start like this:

Bristol, 1st June

Dear Ian,

I went to a fun run last week. ...

Animal Helpline Bristol – Fun run for young and old

◎ **Come and join our fun run in Bristol on 23rd May, 9 am – 3 pm.**

◎ **Find a sponsor for your miles and run as long as you like.**

◎ **Come with all your friends and run 21 miles together.**

◎ **Every mile helps an animal.**

◎ **The money goes directly to Animal Helpline.**

See you on 23rd May!!!

☞ Denke daran, deinen Brief mit einer Grußformel zu beginnen und zu beenden.
   Denke daran, das **simple past** zu verwenden, da du über ein Ereignis in der Vergangenheit schreibst.
   Achte auf die Formen bei den unregelmäßigen Verben.
   Du kannst sie im Buch auf S. 220/221 nachschlagen.

| Gesamtpunktzahl ohne Speaking | _____ / 75 Note _____ |

| Gesamtpunktzahl mit Speaking | _____ / 85 Note _____ |

READING

_____ / 20

This week in your "KIDS' MAGAZINE": PETS

You are looking for a pet? Here is some information for you about guinea pigs, cats and dogs.
It will help you to find the right pet.

HOW TO KEEP YOUR GUINEA PIG HAPPY

Wild guinea pigs live in groups so it's a good idea to keep more than one together. The cage must be big enough so that they can walk around. You can put sawdust[1] on the floor.

It's important to clean the cage every three days. Keep your guinea pigs away from dogs and cats. And don't put the cage in the direct sun. Your guinea pigs want a nice bed, so put some hay[2] into the cage too. Make sure your guinea pigs get enough water: you can put up a bottle in the cage. Your guinea pigs want to run around in your garden. But check that they can't run away. It's best if you buy special guinea pig food.

CATS ARE GOOD TO HAVE

Cats are good pets if they can go outside. Cats love to be in the garden, so it's nice if they can go in and out as they like. But please check that there aren't any dangerous roads.

They like a quiet and warm place, maybe on a sofa. They will sit quietly there and sleep all day. If the weather is good, your cat will lie in a sunny place in your garden. If your cat is hungry, it will walk to its cat bowl. You can buy special cats' food. Your cat must always get enough water. Milk isn't good for your cat.

Sometimes cats are like people: if you do things that your cat doesn't like, it will not be friendly to you. Then it won't look at you for some time. Your cat likes playing. So give it a soft ball to play with, or just a piece of paper or some wool. Your cat likes to play alone.

A DOG CAN BE A GOOD FRIEND

Here are a few ideas to help you and your dog to live together.

The RSPCA say that it costs about £700 a year to look after a dog. Dogs eat different things but they need fresh water every day. Dogs don't want to be alone the whole day and want to run around every day. Let your dog go out in the garden and go for walks with your dog in the park or in the woods as often as you can. So before you buy a dog, you must make sure that you have enough time for your dog every day.

It can be hard work to teach a dog some easy things, but it's good for your dog. You can teach your dog at home or go to dog classes where it can meet other dogs. Your dog will learn to do what you want it to do. Make sure your dog knows its name. This makes teaching easier for you and the dog.

[1] sawdust ['sɔːdʌst] *Sägemehl*   [2] hay [heɪ] *Heu*

1 About the pets

_____ / 7

Look at the pictures. Draw lines from the pet to the things that are important for the pet.
There are more things than you need.

2 What do you know about the pets?

_____ / 13

Use the information from the texts. Tick (✔) the right boxes.
*There are **13 correct** answers.*

	guinea pig	cat	dog
1 It's better to have more than one of them.			
2 You must spend a lot of money on this pet in one year.			
3 It likes the garden.			
4 It needs a bed.			
5 It wants to go for a walk with you.			
6 You can teach it.			
7 It likes sleeping.			
8 This pet likes to be alone.			
9 Be friendly to this pet – or it will not be friendly to you.			
10 Don't leave this pet alone the whole day.			
11 This pet doesn't like the sun.			

LANGUAGE

_____ / 45

1   WORDS Find the words.

_____ / 12

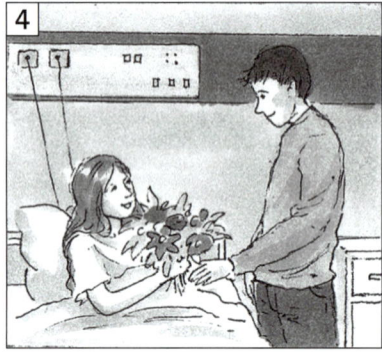 

Find the words and fill them in.

1 The children are playing __ __ ▢ __ __ ▢ __ __ ▢ .

2 Tonight the __ __ __ ▢ is beautiful.

3 What a lot of __ __ __ __ __ ▢ __ __ !

4 Sandra is in the __ __ __ __ __ __ __ . Paul is __ __ __ __ ▢ __ __ __ her.

5 Liam and Peter want to make a __ __ __ ▢ . So they need __ __ __ ▢ .

6 Last month we __ __ __ __ __ __ to London.

7 Mrs Smith is ▢ __ __ __ __ __ __ Susan __ __ __ __ __ __ __ __ __ .

8 Oh __ __ ▢ __ ! The window is __ __ __ __ __ ▢ .

9 Your room must always look ▢ ▢ ▢ ▢ ▢ ▢ ▢ ▢ ▢ ▢ ▢ ▢ .

You can make the expression of **three words** with the letters from the boxes if you put them in the right order.

2   WORDS Say it in English

_____ / 12

Was sagst du, wenn du ...

1   ... jemanden darauf aufmerksam machen möchtest, dass er frieren wird?

_____

2   ... ankündigst, dass du anrufen wirst, sobald du zu Hause bist?

_____

3   ... findest, dass jemand gute Arbeit geleistet hat?

_____

4   ... die Musik eines Freundes nicht ausstehen kannst?

_____

5   ... bedauerst, dass du gehen musst?

_____

6   ... dich über gute Nachrichten freust?

_____

3   GRAMMAR In the pet shop

_____ / 5

Gillian and her mother are in the pet shop. Gillian wants a pet, but she doesn't know which.
Fill in the correct verb forms.

Mrs Brother   Now Gillian, let's look at all the pets.

Gillian   Well, Mum. If I _____ (take) a dog, I will have to go for a walk every morning.

Mrs Brother   Yes, that's right, dear. But if you get up a bit earlier every morning, this _____
(not be) a problem.

Gillian   Hm, I don't know. What about a cat, Mum?

Mrs Brother   Well, if you buy a cat, things _____ (be) easier.

Gillian   You're right. But what can we do if our cat _____ (run) on the road?

Mrs Brother   Yes, that's another big problem. What about a budgie?

Gillian   OK, Mum. I think I'll have the budgie.

Mrs Brother   If you want a budgie, you _____ (clean) the cage. OK?

☞ **Conditional sentences type 1 (Bedingungssätze Typ 1)**

if-Satz	Hauptsatz
simple present	will-future
	must
	can
	Imperativ (Befehl, Aufforderung)

4 GRAMMAR My cat Minky ___/ 12

Last week Amy wrote about her cat Minky.
Complete the text with the correct form of the words in brackets (adjective or adverb).

Minky is a __nice__ (nice) cat. She sits __quietly__ (quiet) on my bed for hours. But if I

don't give her a good lunch, she is __angry__ (angry) and walks away __quickly__ (quick).

She is very __clever__ (clever), too. If she sees a bird she will move __slowly__ (slow), so

that the bird can't see her. When the bird flies away, Minky turns round __angrily__ (angry). Last

year she had five __sweet__ (sweet) babies. She fed them __carefully__ (careful). After two

months we gave them away to some __good__ (good) friends.

I was so __sad__ (sad). But when I saw them play

__happily__ (happy) in my friends' garden it was OK.

☞ **Besonderheiten in der Bildung von Adverbien:**

1 **y** wird zu **i**: angry ▶ angrily
2 **le** wird zu **ly**: terrible ▶ terribly
3 Nach **ic** wird **ally** angehängt: fantastic ▶ fantastically

5 GRAMMAR My dog Norah ___/ 4

*Imagine you have got a dog – Norah. Write **four** sentences about what she does and how she does it.*
*Use the ideas below – use **four** different adjectives and **four** different activities.*

Adjectives:
slow • quick • good • quiet • happy • bad • careful • terrible • fast • ...

Ideas for activities:
say hello • run • bark • do tricks • bring the newspaper • follow the neighbours' cat • ...

☞ Die Adjektive in der Box musst du in Adverbien umwandeln: slow ▶ slow**ly**.

Example:
Norah barks loudly.

1 Norah can run very quickly.
2 Norah does tricks terribly.
3 Norah brings the newspaper fastly.
4 Norah follows the neighbours' cat slowly.

MEDIATION

Finding out about Animal Helpline

Welcome to Bristol Animal Helpline

Who are we?

We are a big organization for animals. We love animals and we want to stop cruelty to animals[1].

Here in Bristol there are the *Animals Home* and the *Animal Clinic*.

Every year we find new families for thousands of animals, like cats, dogs, rabbits, guinea pigs and birds.

We don't get any money from the government[2]. So money is always a problem. We get our money only from sponsors.

Some people like our work but haven't got any money to give to us. These people work here as volunteers. They come to our *Animals Home* and help us with the animals. If you love animals and are looking for a place to help, then just come to *Animal Helpline*. You will like it! We are a really good team!

Every year in June we have a fun run. We get a lot of money from these fun runs. Last year about 800 people ran more than 4000 miles for us. It was one of our happiest days.

Many people give money to us every month or every year. We even get money from young children. They save some of their pocket money every month and happily give it to us. In the year 2007 an old woman won some money in a lottery. She gave us £1000!

If you want to tell us about cruelty to an animal, please call our helpline.

You found this website on the internet. Your uncle works in a pet shop in Germany and is interested in Animal Helpline. He asks you what the website is about.

1   Sag mal, was ist *Animal Helpline*? (2 items)

2   Bekommt diese Organisation Geld von der Regierung oder woher bekommt sie es?

3   Es gibt doch sicherlich viele Leute, die die Arbeit von *Animal Helpline* gut finden,

    aber nicht so viel Geld haben. Wie können diese Leute *Animal Helpline* unterstützen?

4   Was steht da genau über den Sponsorenlauf? (3 items)

5   Wie können Kinder helfen?

6   Und was steht da über die ältere Frau?

7   Wann soll man die Helpline anrufen?

> ☞   Auch wenn du nicht jedes Wort des Textes verstehst, kannst du die Fragen deines Onkels beantworten. Bei manchen Fragen steht 2 oder 3 **items**. Dann musst du 2 oder 3 Fakten zur Beantwortung der Frage beitragen.

---

[1] cruelty to animals [ˈkruːəlti] *Tierquälerei*   [2] government [ˈgʌvənmənt] *Regierung*

SPEAKING

_____/ 10

🎧 09 An interview about pets

The presenter of Bristol Today is interviewing Alan about his pet. Listen to the interview.

🎧 10 Now you

Now the presenter is interviewing you. First make notes about your pet:

your pet: (1P)	
he/she, name? (1P)	
what's special? (3 items) (3P)	
who feeds / **what food?** (2P)	
parents: help? (2 items) (2P)	
holidays? (1P)	

Now listen to the speaker's questions and answer them.

Gesamtpunktzahl _____ / 66   Note _____

READING

_____ / 23

 Es ist oft sinnvoll, die Aufgaben vor dem Text gründlich durchzulesen. Dann weißt du, worauf du beim Lesen des Textes achten musst und du kannst die Aufgaben gleich beim Lesen bearbeiten. Dann siehst du, dass es auch nicht so schlimm ist, wenn du nicht jedes Wort verstehst, weil du die Aufgaben trotzdem lösen kannst.

BBC[1] Wales Bus on tour

The BBC Wales Bus was on tour again last week, when it visited Valley School in Carmarthenshire in Wales. It stopped there for two days. The bus has 20 computers on board where the students can work. They can surf the internet, download pictures and music, work on projects and chat with friends or send them e-mails. But the most interesting part is always the small radio studio on the bus.

Students from Year 5–7 were very excited. They got into groups to visit the big red bus, and worked on different tasks[2].

Year 5 started on Monday morning. Their task was to work on the topic "My way to school". First everybody worked alone to find out about questions like: How far is it to school? Are there any dangerous roads? Must I go by bus or can I walk? Some of the students even made maps[3] on the computer to describe their way to school. Then they reported to the other students. The results were interesting.

On Monday afternoon it was Year 6's turn. They practised presentations because they wanted to get better. They practised with cameras. This was difficult because it was the first time for most students. But they knew how important it is to learn to give better presentations. So they worked hard. Then they watched the films, talked about the presentations and made them better.

Year 7 was on the bus on Tuesday morning. Their task was to prepare a school trip to Cardiff. They surfed the internet for information. One group found out about museums in Cardiff. A second group looked for information about how to get wool[4] from sheep. Group 3 collected ideas for an interesting day trip to Caerphilly Castle with its leaning tower. And the last group found out about the train times and how much a return ticket[5] is.

And on Tuesday afternoon? On Tuesday afternoon the small radio studio was open for all the students. And everybody could ask for their favourite song on the radio. That was great! Everybody had fun on the BBC Wales Bus.

---

[1] BBC = **B**ritish **B**roadcasting **C**orporation *britischer Radio- und Fernsehsender*   [2] task [tɑːsk] *Aufgabe*
[3] map [maep] *(Land-)Karte*   [4] wool [wʊl] *Wolle*   [5] return ticket [rɪ'tɜːn ˌtɪkɪt] *Rückfahrkarte*

1 The BBC Wales Bus and the students

_____ / 14

Fill in the chart with the information from the text: one fact for each bullet point •.

	Year 5	Year 6	Year 7	Everybody
When?	• _____	• _____	• _____	• _____
What was their topic?	• _____ _____	• _____	• _____	open for everybody
What did they do?	• _____ _____ • _____ _____	• _____ • _____	• _____ • _____	• _____ _____

2 After the visit to the BBC Bus

_____ / 9

After their visit to the BBC Bus the students talked about it. Who said what?
Write the numbers of the statements into the speech bubbles of Megan, David and Abby.

Megan, Year 5

David, Year 6

Abby, Year 7

1 "It was hard to talk in front of the camera."

2 "A group ticket to Cardiff is …"

3 "When I give a presentation, I'm not nervous now."

4 "I didn't know that it is three miles from my house to school."

5 "I have to be careful when I ride my bike to school."

6 "It was so funny when Mike suddenly laughed and couldn't stop any more."

7 "There are some really nice restaurants in Cardiff where you can get a cheap lunch."

8 "I can read maps[1] now."

9 "The last train back to Cardiff is at 10.30."

[1] map [mæp] *(Land-)Karte*

LANGUAGE

 ____ / 29

1 GRAMMAR What have they just done?

____ / 7

a) Look at the notes. Write down what they have just done.

1   Caroline – write an e-mail

_____

2   Jenny and Anna – find information about Caerphilly Castle

_____

3   Martin – look at the timetable

_____

4   Sue – read about a museum in Cardiff

_____

b) Now you

What have you already done today? / What haven't you done yet?
*Write at least **three** sentences and use the present perfect.*

> ☞   Denke daran, für das **present perfect** have/has + die dritte Form zu verwenden.
>   Bei unregelmäßigen Verben ist die dritte Form natürlich auch unregelmäßig: eat – ate – eaten.

2 WORDS Describing a picture

____ / 10

a) Look at the picture and write down the words. (4P)

1   _____

2   _____

3   _____

4   _____

5   _____

6   _____

7   _____

8   _____

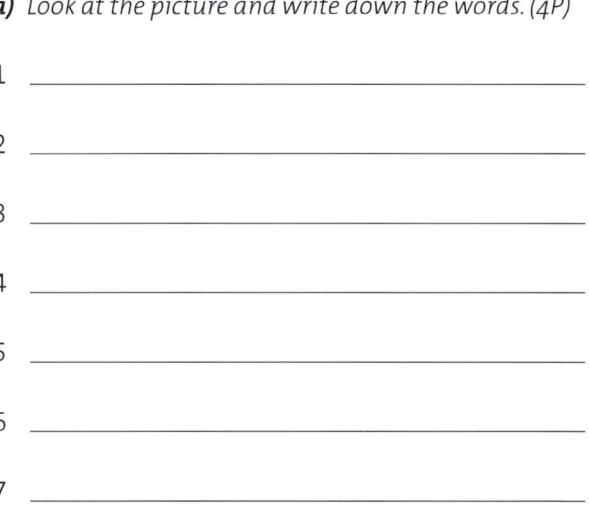

b) Now describe the picture in complete sentences. Start with the foreground and then go to the background. Find a topic sentence (= einleitender Satz) for your text. (6P)

> ☞   Wichtige Hinweise zu **nützlichen Wörtern** und zur richtigen **Verwendung der Zeiten** bei
>   **Bildbeschreibungen** findest du im Klassenarbeitstrainer auf S. 11.
>   Hilfen, wie du einen **topic sentence** formulieren kannst, findest du im **Skills File** in deinem
>   Englischbuch auf S. 123.

3   WORDS Opposites

_____ / 6

a) *Find the opposites of these words:*

1   husband   ◀▶ _____   4   quiet   ◀▶ _____

2   strong   ◀▶ _____   5   valley   ◀▶ _____

3   dirty   ◀▶ _____   6   exciting   ◀▶ _____

b) *Find three more opposites:*

1   _____   ◀▶   _____

2   _____   ◀▶   _____

3   _____   ◀▶   _____

4   STUDY SKILLS How to give a good presentation

_____ / 6

Here are three paragraphs:

a) *Put the sentences of each paragraph (♣ ♦ ♠) in the right order. Write the letters next to the numbers.*

♣   [A] You should only have a few key words on your cards.

[B] First you must say what you are talking about.

[C] Then start with your information.

[D] Don't read out your text.

1 ☐   2 ☐   3 ☐   4 ☐

♦   [A] Then wait till everybody is quiet.

[B] Before you start talking, prepare everything you need.

[C] A good presentation needs good preparation[1].

[D] Hang up posters, get the projector ready.

1 ☐   2 ☐   3 ☐   4 ☐

♠   [A] Then ask for questions.

[B] When you show pictures, you must always explain them.

[C] At the end of the presentation you should say that you have finished.

[D] Look at your listeners as often as you can.

1 ☐   2 ☐   3 ☐   4 ☐

b) *Find the first, the second and the third paragraph. The topic sentence helps you to find the first paragraph.*

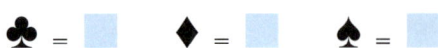

♣ = ☐   ♦ = ☐   ♠ = ☐

---

[1] preparation [prepə'reɪʃn] *Vorbereitung*

MEDIATION

_____ / 14

Where can we go?

You are staying at a camping site[1] in Wales together with your parents. You and your parents want to plan some day trips. So you go to the tourist information centre to get some information. Because your parents don't speak very much Welsh or English you help with the conversation.

Your mum   Sag ihr bitte, dass wir hier auf dem Campingplatz wohnen und gerne einige Tagesausflüge planen möchten. Frag sie dann bitte, ob sie uns ein paar Tipps geben kann.

You   Good morning. We are staying _____

You   _____

Woman   Yes, of course. There are many things to do here. But first let me ask you:
Do you want to visit museums or do you want to go to the beach?

You   Sie sagt, dass _____

You   _____

Your mum   Das ist schwierig zu beantworten. Wenn die Sonne scheint und es warm ist, gehen wir an den Strand. Aber wir brauchen auch Ideen für schlechtes Wetter. Wir könnten in ein oder zwei Museen gehen, finde ich.

You   _____

_____

You   _____

Woman   OK. I understand. On this map here you can see all the beaches near the camping site.
I mark these two nice beaches for you on the map. You will like them.

You   Also, auf dieser Karte _____

You   _____

Woman   Now, if the weather is bad, there are many small museums.
Here is a brochure with all the information.

You   _____

You   _____

Your mum   Das sind ja tolle Ideen. Bedank dich bitte und frag noch gleich nach einem guten Café.

You   _____

Woman   Yes, you can go to the Red Dragon. That's very good. Bye-bye and have nice trips.

Your mum   Also, das habe ich jetzt auch verstanden. Thank you very much and bye-bye.

[1] camping site ['kæmpɪŋ saɪt] *Campingplatz*

Gesamtpunktzahl ohne Speaking	_____ / 70 Note _____
Gesamtpunktzahl mit Speaking	_____ / 85 Note _____

LISTENING

_____ / 22

🎧11 **Three reports on an accident**

There has been an accident. The police talk to a boy, a woman and a man. Listen to what they say.

> **New word**
> light [laɪt] *Licht*

1   About the accident

_____ / 6

Listen and match the photos to the information. Draw lines.

boy   has a shock

woman   called the police

man   was a bit late

2 More facts about the accident   ____/ 16

Read the chart first. Then listen again and find the different facts.

	The boy's story	The woman's story	The man's story
lights on the boy's bike: yes/no?			
the boy's bike: slow/fast?			
the boy's clothes			
the woman's car: fast/slow?			
the boy's injuries[1]		✕	
Who called the paramedics?	✕		

LANGUAGE   ____/ 35

1 WORDS irregular verbs   ____/ 10

Fill in the missing forms.

Infinitive	Simple past form	Past participle	German translation
(to) be			
(to) eat			
(to) find			
(to) go			
(to) come			
(to) have			
(to) take			
(to) make			
(to) do			
(to) see			

[1] injury ['ɪndʒəri] *Verletzung*

2   GRAMMAR After the accident

_____ / 9

An accident has just happened in Leicester Road. Read the notes and write down
what the people have done or haven't done yet. Write one sentence for each note.
*Be careful where you put the words **already**, **yet**, **just** (siehe Hinweisbox).*

1   Alan – phone – the police

_____

2   the paramedics – take the boy – to hospital

_____

3   two policemen – talk to – the man

_____

4   the policemen – not write – the report

_____

5   the driver of the car – not visit – the boy in hospital

_____

6   the policemen – phone – the boy's parents   just

_____

 Die **Bildung des present perfect** kannst du dir in Erinnerung rufen, wenn du dir den Lerntipp
auf S. 30 oben in den **Lösungen** ansiehst.

already = schon, **not … yet** = noch nicht, **just** = gerade eben
Solche Adverbien der unbestimmten Zeit findest du oft in *present perfect*-Sätzen.
Sie stehen in der Regel direkt vor dem *past participle*: *I've **already** parked the car.*
Ausnahme: *yet* steht am Satzende: *I haven't seen Dan **yet**.*

3   WORDS At the doctor's

_____ / 6

The following people are sitting in Dr Smith's waitingroom. Everybody has a different problem.
Write what's wrong with them.

1   Mr Miller has _____ .

2   John _____ .

3   Sally _____ .

4   Mr Baker _____ .

5   Susan _____ .

6   Mrs Marple _____ .

4   GRAMMAR Mum and Dad have got a lot of questions

_____ / 5

When the boy's parents visit him in hospital they have got a lot of questions.
Form the questions and write them down.

1	you	visit you
2	the driver of the car	read the new book
3	the doctor	write you an e-mail
4	your teacher	see you
5	your friends	phone Grandma
6	you	bring you the homework

1   *Have you phoned Grandma?*

2   _____

3   _____

4   _____

5   _____

6   _____

5   GRAMMAR Where will they be when?

_____ / 5

Write sentences where the boys and girls will be when. Think of place before time.

Ort vor Zeit

1   Natale – next Monday

2   Isabel – tomorrow

3   Barry – next weekend

4   Tracy and Terry – in the afternoon

5   Adam – in a few minutes

1   *Natale will be* _____ .

2   _____

3   _____

4   _____

5   _____

WRITING

$\boxed{ / 13}$

Mike's letter to his grandma

Mike is in hospital after his accident. He is writing a letter to his grandma.
He writes about:

– when and where the accident was
– what happened
– the paramedics
– what's wrong with him and how he feels
– what it is like in hospital
– how long he must stay in hospital
– who visits him and what they bring
– when he can go home from hospital

Write a beginning and an ending.

 In dieser Schreibübung musst du verschiedene Zeiten verwenden

Überlege daher vorher:
- [ ] Hat das, worüber ich schreiben will, in der Vergangenheit stattgefunden
  - ▶ **simple past** *(Last Wednesday I went …)*
- [ ] Beschreibt das, worüber ich schreiben will, einen momentanen Zustand oder findet es regelmäßig statt?
  - ▶ **simple present** *(I have a terrible headache. / My parents visit me every day.)*
- [ ] Findet das, worüber ich schreiben will, erst in der Zukunft statt
  - ▶ **will-future** *(I will go home tomorrow).*

SPEAKING

$\boxed{ / 15}$

🎧 12 **School paramedics**

Manuel is an exchange student from Essen, Germany. At his school in Germany he is a school paramedic.
He explains what school paramedics at his school do. Listen to Manuel.

🎧 13 **Now you**

Bessy wants to do an interview with Manuel for the school radio. Imagine you are Manuel and answer Bessy's questions.
Listen to Bessy's questions and use the pictures for your answers.

- [ ] Höre dir Bessys Fragen zuerst einmal an. Schaue dir dazu die Bilder an.
  Erinnere dich daran, was Manuel über seine Aufgabe als Schulsanitäter berichtet hat.
  Überlege, wie du die Fragen beantworten kannst.
- [ ] Höre dir dann die Fragen ein zweites Mal an und beantworte sie.
  Halte dabei den Text an, damit du Zeit für deine Antworten hast.

Year 7–9

Tuesday afternoon – six weeks –
told about work, what they can/can't do

hurt students – sometimes call Essen paramedics

Bessy Who are the new school paramedics and what years are they from?

You …

Bessy Who did the training with you?

You …

Bessy When was the training and what did you learn?

You …

Bessy How can the school paramedics help?

You …

Bessy When and where can students find you?

You …

Unit 5   Klassenarbeit A

© 2008 Cornelsen Verlag, Berlin. Alle Rechte vorbehalten.

| Gesamtpunktzahl _____ / 65   Note _____ |

LISTENING

____ / 17

 14 **A great team: the "Shocking Smoothies"**

The Cotham School kids are talking about the BigBanana juice bar and they have got an idea.
Listen to Alex, Julie, Kerry and Ralph.

New word
head teacher [ˌhed ˈtiːtʃə] *Schulleiter/in*

☞ Lies dir vor dem Hören die Aufgabe genau durch. Dann weißt du, worauf du beim Hören achten musst und du wirst feststellen, dass du die Aufgaben lösen kannst, auch wenn du nicht jedes Wort verstehst.

1   Smoothies at school

____ / 8

*Look at the pictures. Listen to the text. You must tick (✔) **eight** things that the kids are talking about.*

2   More about the smoothies bar

____ / 9

Read the following statements. Then listen again and tick (✔) the correct box.

		Right	Wrong
1	Alex liked the strawberry smoothie in the bar.		
2	They want to go to the bar again tomorrow afternoon.		
3	Kerry thinks that smoothies at school are too difficult.		
4	They don't need to ask the head teacher.		
5	They want to give all the money to Animal Helpline.		
6	They already know the price for one smoothie.		
7	The Smoothies team must clean the dirty glasses.		
8	They want to hang up posters.		
9	They can't find a name for their bar.		

LANGUAGE

/ 30

1 GETTING BY IN ENGLISH Say it in English

/ 7

Was sagst du, wenn ...

1 du jemanden darauf aufmerksam machen möchtest, dass er/sie in die falsche Richtung geht?

_____

2 du denkst, dass jemand etwas nicht ernst meint oder Witze macht?

_____

3 dein Mitspieler ein Feld zurückgehen soll?

_____

4 du ausdrücken willst: „Alles, was wir jetzt noch tun müssen, ist einfach."?

_____

5 du etwas nicht kapierst?

_____

6 du jemanden fragen möchtest, was du ihm bringen kannst?

_____

7 du ein Lied ziemlich gut findest?

_____

2 WORDS Plural of nouns

/ 4

Write down the plural of the nouns.

1 one dice   two _____

2 one strawberry two _____

3 one thief   two _____

4 one wolf   two _____

5 one man   two _____

6 one woman   two _____

7 one child   two _____

8 one sheep   two _____

3 GRAMMAR Who is doing what?

_____ / 4

You are talking to a friend from another school.
You want to tell your friend what the students are doing and what their names are.
*Look at the pictures and make sentences with **who**.*

> **New word**
> head teacher [ˌhed ˈtiːtʃə] *Schulleiter/in*

two boys – Mike and Alex

two girls – Julie and Liz

boy – Ralph

boy and girl – Julie and Alex

two boys – Alex and Kerry

Example:

1 The two boys who are working out the price for the smoothies are Mike and Alex.

2 _____

3 _____

4 _____

5 _____

> ☞ Das Relativpronomen *who* steht in Relativsätzen, die **Personen** beschreiben:
> **The student/woman/people** *who ...*

4 GRAMMAR The Shocking Smoothies Bar is open

_____ /7

Complete the sentences with question tags.

Sally Let's have a smoothie, Sue. The Shocking Smoothies Bar is a great idea, _isn't it_ ?

Sue It is, yes. But now I'd like to try one. What flavour would you like?

Sally I don't know, really. They are all good, _aren't they_ ?

The strawberry flavour is delicious, _isn't it_ ?

Sue They use fresh strawberries, ~~~~ _don't they_ ?

Sally I think they have got the best strawberry smoothie here, _haven't they_ ?

Sue Yes, they even won a prize for it, _didn't they_ ?

Sally It was last year, _wasn't it_ ?

👉   Aussagesatz bejaht ▸ question tag verneint
Aussagesatz verneint ▸ question tag bejaht
Benutze Farben zum Unterstreichen:
grün für die bejahte Form und rot für die verneinte Form: Das Verb im Hauptsatz und
im question tag müssen immer unterschiedliche Farben haben.

Denke an die Hilfverben don't/doesn't/didn't in den question tags.
(Sophie likes healthy food ▸ **doesn't** she?)

5 STUDY SKILLS New attraction: Healthy but good

_____ /8

You have read an article on the website of Cotham School about their smoothies bar.
Your friends are asking you about this attraction: Read your friends' questions:

1 What's special about the smoothies?
2 Are the smoothies expensive?
3 When do they sell the smoothies?
4 Does their head teacher like your idea?

First find the four facts in the text for your answers and mark them. Then answer the questions in sentences.

Cotham School

Healthy but good
New attraction at Cotham School in Bristol

A group of students of Cotham School has just worked out a new attraction: everybody can get healthy and delicious smoothies at lunch break now. The Smoothies Team makes the smoothies and sells them at a cheap price. They are going to give some of the money to the Animal Helpline and spend the rest on the next school trip. The head teacher thinks that the idea shows good teamwork. "We got the idea when we tried the delicious smoothies in a juice bar. We understood that good food can be healthy too," says Sophie, one of the Smoothies team.

WRITING

____/ 18

An e-mail to the Shocking Smoothies Team

You have read an article on the website of Cotham School about their smoothies bar. You like the idea and want to find out more about the smoothies project, because you and your friends want to open a smoothies bar at your school too.

Write an e-mail to the Shocking Smoothies team and ask for details. The notes will help you.
Don't forget to write a beginning and an ending.

e-mail to Cotham School:
- read article on the internet
- like your idea
- open smoothies bar at our school
- many questions
- how – start?
- students – how many?
- price?
- problems?
- ask head teacher – before you started?
- glasses?
- send – recipe[1]

Fragen mit do/does/did:
Do you read many books?
Does John like cake?
Did you go to the milk bar yesterday?
How often do you go to the swimming pool?

Denke auch an folgende Möglichkeiten
Fragen zu beginnen:
What about ...?
Could you ...?
How much/many ...?

_____

_____

_____

_____

_____

_____

_____

_____

_____

[1] recipe ['resəpi] *Rezept*

© 2008 Cornelsen Verlag, Berlin. Alle Rechte vorbehalten.

Gesamtpunktzahl ohne Speaking	_____ / 70 Note _____
Gesamtpunktzahl mit Speaking	_____ / 80 Note _____

READING

_____ / 12

New games for everybody

Last week was very exciting for the students of 6 PF. Mr Fisher divided the class into eight teams. Every team had to invent[1] a new board game. A difficult task!

First the children brought their board games from home. The teams found out how you play the different games and played them. So they learned how you must write the instructions for a board game. They also talked about what colours you must use so that the games look interesting and exciting.

Every team found a special topic for their game. Then they started to make their game. It was a lot of work and every student in the team had a job. They drew their game, then some coloured the board, some made nice counters and dice and all the other things that they needed for their games. They needed a lot of glue, scissors and paper. The instructions were the most difficult job. You must write them clearly so that every player understands the game. In the end they even made a box for their game, painted it and wrote the name on top.

After many hours of work the games were ready. The games had all different names, sometimes they were funny too. Here are some of the names: _At the Zoo, Up and down High Street, Isidor and the Market, The Great Harbour Game, Asterix and Obelix_ and _A Funny Tour around the School._

When all the games were ready, they played all of them because they wanted to find "The best game of 6 PF". It was difficult because all the games were good. So they had to look at the colours of the game, the instructions and if the game was exciting. In the end "The Great Harbour Game" with all its colourful ships was the winner. Congratulations!

1 Headings

_____ / 5

Here are five headings. Match the headings and the five paragraphs. Draw lines.

paragraph 1   a) Lots of interesting games

paragraph 2   b) Finding the super game

paragraph 3   c) Making groups

paragraph 4   d) Making a new game

paragraph 5   e) Playing games from home

[1] (to) invent [ɪnˈvent] _erfinden_

2 About the week of the games ____/7

Read the sentences. Then tick (✔) the correct box.

		Right	Wrong	Not in the text
1	The students of 6PF invented a new game together.	☐	☐	☐
2	Every team got a topic from Mr Fisher.	☐	☐	☐
3	Everybody in the team had a job.	☐	☐	☐
4	At the beginning some teams had problems.	☐	☐	☐
5	They also made coloured boxes.	☐	☐	☐
6	The instructions of the games weren't clear.	☐	☐	☐
7	The students of the best game got a present.	☐	☐	☐

LANGUAGE ____/40

1 WORDS Find the words. ____/9

Find the words and fill them in.

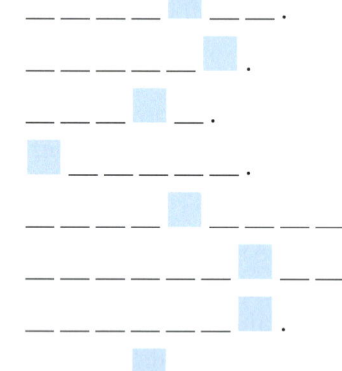

1 Smoothies are good and ＿ ＿ ＿ ＿ ☐ ＿ ＿ .

2 The opposite of leave is ＿ ＿ ＿ ＿ ＿ ☐ .

3 It makes your tea sweet: ＿ ＿ ＿ ☐ ＿ .

4 You can buy fresh fruit there: ☐ ＿ ＿ ＿ ＿ ＿ .

5 It's a sweet little red fruit: ＿ ＿ ＿ ＿ ☐ ＿ ＿ ＿ ＿ .

6 The smoothie is super. It's ＿ ＿ ＿ ＿ ＿ ＿ ＿ ☐ ＿ ＿ .

7 You need this to play a board game: ＿ ＿ ＿ ＿ ＿ ＿ ☐ ＿ .

8 A small book with information is a ＿ ＿ ＿ ☐ ＿ ＿ ＿ .

Now you

Can you explain the word from the boxes?

☐ ☐ ☐ ☐ ☐ ☐ ☐ is when ＿＿＿＿＿＿＿＿＿＿＿＿＿＿＿＿＿＿＿＿

＿＿＿＿＿＿＿＿＿＿＿＿＿＿＿＿＿＿＿＿＿＿＿＿＿＿＿＿＿＿＿＿＿＿＿

2 GRAMMAR Plans for the game

_____ / 5

*Mr Fisher is asking the different teams about their games. Write down his questions with **going to**.*

 Fragen mit going to:

Mit Fragewort: What are you going to do next?
Ohne Fragewort: Is he going to sing another song?

3   you – help – John with the counters

2   Peter – work on – the instructions

4   you ~~make~~ – a box for your game

1   you – make – a game about animals

5   when – you – show – the game – to the class

1 _____

2 _____

3 _____

4 _____

5 _____

3 WORDS The Great Harbour Game

_____ / 7

While[1] the teams are making their games they are talking a lot about the game.
Complete their dialogue with:

some • any • something • somewhere • somebody • anywhere • anybody

 some und die mit **some** zusammengesetzten Wörter stehen vor allem in bejahten Sätzen.
any und die mit **any** zusammengesetzten Wörter stehen vor allem in verneinten Sätzen
und Fragen.

Sue   I need _____ help. Can _____ help me please?

Mike   OK. How can I help?

Sue   Well, I'm drawing the board. I haven't got _____ good ideas for the pictures.

Mike   What about pirates?

Sue   That's a good idea.   →

[1] while [waɪl] *während*

Liz   I can't find our ideas for the instructions. They must be _____.

Sue   I've already looked for them and I couldn't see them _____.

Mike   Oh, come on girls, _____ must have them.

Phil   Here they are. Jill and I have added _____.

4 GRAMMAR Are the games ready?

_____ / 4

Look at the list. Say what the students have done or haven't done for their games.

all the students	learn how to write the instructions for a game ✔
Sue	paint the board ✘
Phil	write the instructions ✘
Mike and Jill	make six counters ✔
Liz	paint the box and write the name on it ✔

Example: *All the students have learned how to write the instructions for the game.*

1 _____

2 _____

3 _____

4 _____

5 GRAMMAR How they worked

_____ / 6

Write how they worked in their teams. Fill in the missing adverbs of manner.

John read the instructions of the game _____ (quick).

The teams worked on their games very _____ (hard).

Tim and Sandra talked about the game _____ (quiet).

The team presented their game _____ (proud).

Now you

Think of what you did yesterday. Then write two sentences how you did it.
Use adjectives from the box as adverbs of manner

slow • angry • terrible • good • fast • nice • rude

1 _____

2 _____

6 GRAMMAR All the games are ready now

_____ / 4

Write about the games and the students who made the games. Use **who** *or* **which**.

1 Sophie – the girl – drew the nicest board

Sophie is the girl _____

2 "At the Zoo" – a game – is for six players

_____

3 Marc, Ian and John – the boys – made "Up and down High Street"

_____

4 little bananas and apples – counters – you need for the game

_____

7 GRAMMAR More about the games

_____ / 5

Match the correct sentence halves and combine them with **who**, **which** *or* **whose**.

1 "At the Zoo" is the game ...

2 Jill, Sue, Mike and Phil are the students ...

3 Molly is the girl ...

4 Colourful ships are the counters ...

5 Steve is the boy ...

a) He made a really good box.

b) Her ideas helped a lot to make the "Great Harbour Game".

c) It shows you many animals from Africa.

d) Their game is 6PF's best game.

e) They are part of the "Great Harbour Game".

1 _____

_____

2 _____

_____

3 _____

_____

4 _____

_____

5 _____

_____

MEDIATION

© 2008 Cornelsen Verlag, Berlin. Alle Rechte vorbehalten.

_____ / 18

A new game: The terrible red dragon

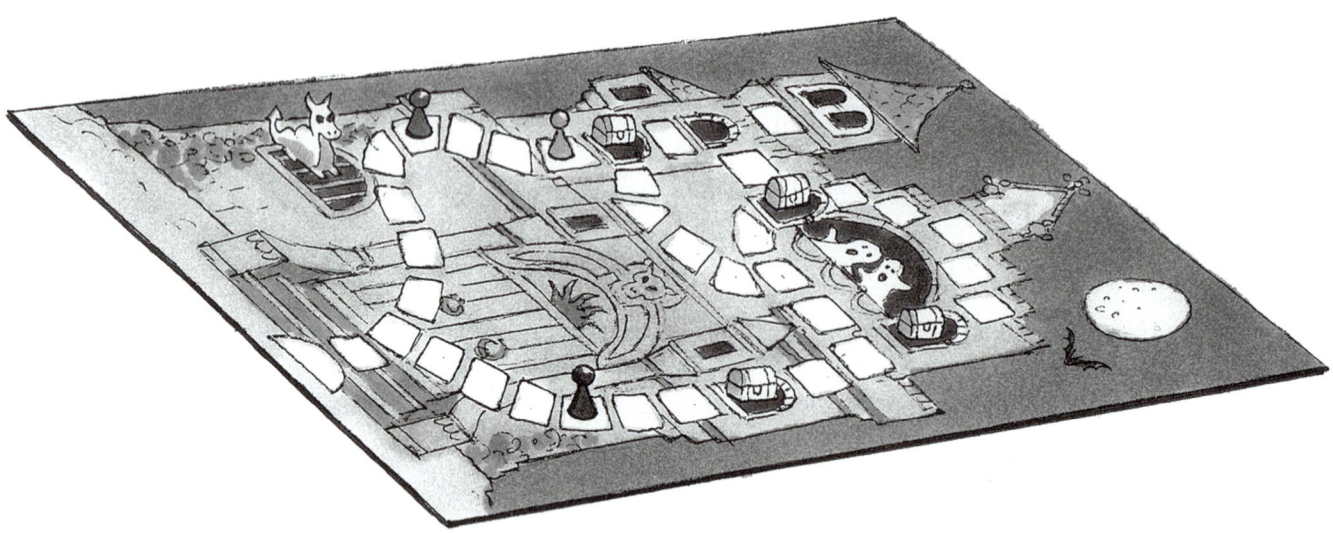

The terrible red dragon

Number of players:	3 – 5
Age:	10 – 99 years
Time:	about 40 minutes
You need:	a dice, a counter for each player, the board and twelve boxes of gold, the red dragon
Idea of the game:	In a castle a hungry dragon is waiting to eat the players. The players are in the castle because they want to find as much gold as possible. The way through the castle is long and dangerous.
How to start:	Put the counters to the start position. The terrible dragon looks at them. The youngest player throws the dice first. If he/she throws a four he/she can start.
The spaces:	If you land on a brown space you miss a turn. If you land on a golden space you throw again and collect one box of gold. If you land on a black space the dragon moves one space nearer. If you land on a red space you must pay one box of gold to the dragon.
The dragon:	If the dragon lands on your counter it will eat you.
The winner:	If you get to the top of the castle and if you have the most boxes of gold you are the winner.

Your sister got a new game for her birthday. The instructions are in English. You help her.
Explain how to play the game.

Erkläre deiner Schwester:

1 wie viele Spieler in welchem Alter mitspielen können   (2P)
2 was man alles zum Spiel benötigt   (3P)
3 die Idee des Spiels   (3P)
4 wie man beginnt   (2P)
5 die Bedeutung der verschiedenen Felder   (4P)
6 die Rolle des Drachens   (2P)
7 wann man gewonnen hat   (2P)

SPEAKING

🎧 15 **Let's present our new game**

The students of Form 6 PF have invented new games. Now all teams present their game to the class.
Listen to the first team.

New word
board [bɔːd] *Spielbrett*

Now you

You worked in one of the other teams. Now you present your game to the class.
You can choose a name from the box or think of a new name.

At the Zoo • Up and down High Street • A Funny Tour around the School •
The Great Animal Party • The Round Britain Game • ...

Make notes of what you are going to say before you speak.

You must talk about:	Your ideas:
name of the game (1P)	
who was on your team? (1P)	
how many players? how old? (1P)	
what you need for the game (1P)	
idea of the game (2P)	
what is special (red space, green space, questions, ...)? (2P)	
who is the winner? (2P)	

Gesamtpunktzahl ohne Speaking	_____ / 55 Note _____
Gesamtpunktzahl mit Speaking	_____ / 70 Note _____

READING   _____ / 14

 Oft geht es bei Reading-Aufgaben darum, einen Text gezielt nach Informationen abzusuchen **(Scanning)**. Deshalb ist es sehr wichtig, dass du zunächst die Aufgabe durchliest. Dann kannst du ganz gezielt nach den gefragten Informationen suchen und brauchst nur dort genauer nachlesen, wo du sie findest.

BATH – Daily News   *Wednesday, 15th July*

Visitors in Bath

It's summertime – and this means that there are lots of visitors in Bath.
Our reporter Helen Fields talked to some of them yesterday afternoon.

First time

Hello, my name is Philip Smith and this is my wife. Well, we are just here for the day. At the moment we are on holiday. But we decided to stay at home and just go on day trips. So the holidays are not so expensive because we can  sleep at home in Gloucester. Yesterday we went to Wales and today we visited the Roman Baths. It's our first time here in Bath and we like it very much. We want to come again and visit the Museum of Costume.

A bike ride to Bath

I'm Susan from Bristol. I'm here with my mum because we want to do some shopping. Yes, I'm on holiday at the moment, well, there is no school, so today we cycled to Bath. It's quite easy to cycle from Bristol to Bath. We've been 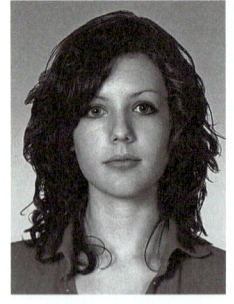 here lots of times before: we have visited the Roman Baths and the William Herschel Museum. Today we are only going shopping and then cycling home. But at the weekend my parents and I want to visit the Museum of Costume.

Romans in Bath and Heitersheim, Germany

My name is Helen Günter and I am from Germany. I'm on holiday with my two daughters Anna and Lea. Yesterday we flew from Stuttgart to London and then we went to Bath by train. I came to Bath when I was about  15 years old. Now I want to show the Roman Baths to my daughters. You see, there is an old Roman villa in Heitersheim, the town in Germany where we come from, so the girls really wanted to see the Roman Baths here in Bath. This evening we will take the train to Scotland.

Learning English

Hola, I'm José. I'm Spanish and I come from Madrid. I'm here for three weeks and I'm learning English at a language school in Bath. We are 20 students from all over the world. We have lessons in the morning and in the  afternoon. But Wednesday afternoon is free. Last Wednesday we went to London. This afternoon my friends and I want to visit the Roman Baths. For next Wednesday we're planning to visit Bristol. No, I've never been to Bath before.

Find out about the different visitors

_____ / 14

Take notes of all the information about the different people.

	Philip Smith	Helen Günter	Susan	José
where from?				
in Bath alone / together with?				
how long in Bath?				
in Bath for the first time[1]?				
activities in the past this week				
activities today				
activities in the next days				

LANGUAGE

_____ / 29

1   WORDS In the city

_____ / 10

_a)_ _Think of buildings and places in the city. Find at least ten. Be careful with your spelling. (5P)_

1 _____   6 _____

2 _____   7 _____

3 _____   8 _____

4 _____   9 _____

5 _____   10 _____

[1] for the first time _zum ersten Mal_

b) *What do you say when you want to tell somebody the way? (5P)*

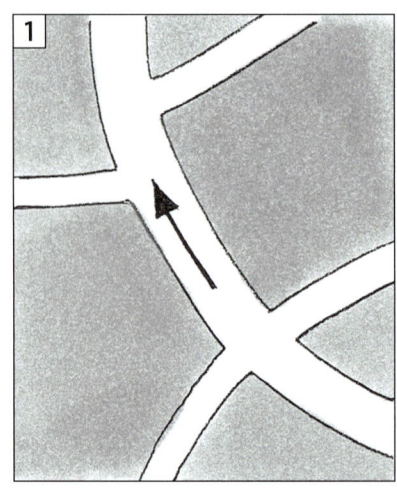
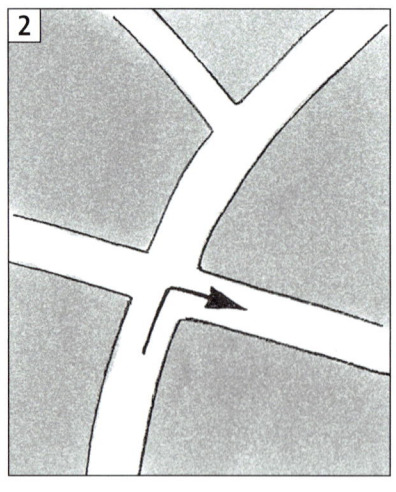
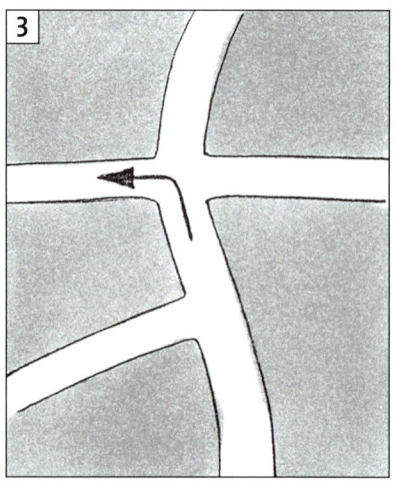

1 _____   2 _____   3 _____

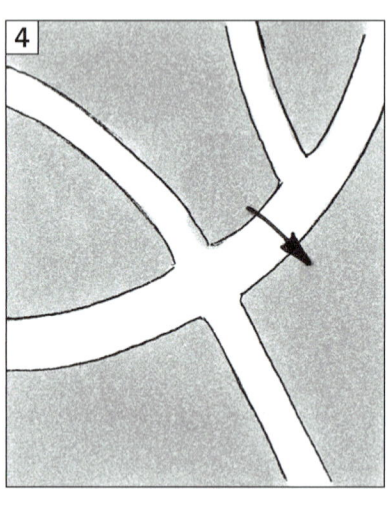
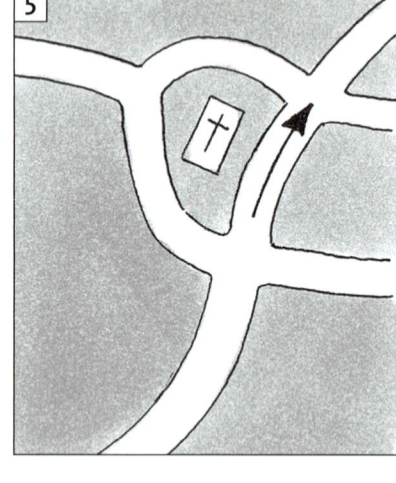

4 _____   5 _____

2   WORDS   Find the words.   _____/7

Find the words and fill them in.

1   One hundred years are a

2   You can watch plays in a

3   When you are very tired, you must often

4   When two people talk they have a

5   In Britain the school year has three

6   William Herschel

____ ____ ____ ____ ____ ____ ____ ____ ____ Uranus.

7   If you put the letters in the boxes in the right order you get a word for the people who act in a play.

3 WORDS About the tourists in Bath

_____ / 6

Underline the correct prepositions.

1 Susan and her mother are sitting **on**/**off**/**at** a table in a café.

2 They will cycle back **for**/**to**/**after** Bristol.

3 José wants to have a look **to**/**for**/**at** the Roman Baths too.

4 **At**/**On**/**In** 5 o'clock he wants to visit the Roman Baths with his friends.

5 Many visitors want to see the old costumes **in**/**at**/**by** the Museum of Costumes.

6 **On**/**At**/**Off** Wednesdays it is open until 10 pm.

4 GRAMMAR What are they doing?

_____ / 6

Write down what the people in the picture are doing.
These verbs will help you. There are two more than you need.

write • visit • sit • ask • learn • go shopping • wait • play

1 Mr and Mrs Smith _____.

2 A girl _____.

3 Susan and her mother _____.

4 Mrs Günter and her daughters _____.

5 José _____.

6 A woman _____.

> **Present progressive:**
>
> **So wird es gebildet:**
>
> | I am | | I am writing a letter. |
> | you/they/we are | + **ing**-Form: | We are playing football. |
> | he/she/it is | | He is reading a book. |
>
> **So wird es verwendet:**
>
> Das **Present progressive** wird verwendet, wenn man ausdrücken will,
> dass etwas gerade geschieht.

MEDIATION

_____ / 12

Get to know Bath – Come and enjoy our bus tours

Why not go sightseeing in Bath by bus? It's the easiest way to see our beautiful city. The tour takes about one hour.

There is a lot you can see:

No visit in Bath without going to the Roman Baths!

You will also see the oldest house in Bath (from 1483), the Museum of Costume, the William Herschel House, our famous Royal Victoria Park and the Circus – a round road.

You can start the tour at all the stops. Just look at the map, you'll find every stop there.

If you want to visit one of our museums or have a look at the park, just get off and get on the next bus again. There is a guide on every bus who will explain everything to you and answer all your questions.

Hours

First bus leaves at 9.30 am, last bus at 5 pm.

1st April to 30th November: sightseeing buses run every day.

1st December to 31st March: sightseeing buses run at the weekends only.

You can get off at every stop, visit the museum or the park and then get on the bus again.

More information:

Prices:
Adults: £ 5.99
or: £ 11 (including ticket for Roman Baths)

Children 5–14: £ 2.99
or: £ 8 (including ticket for Roman Baths)

Children under 5: free

Family tickets: £ 15
or: £ 30 (including ticket for Roman Baths)

Tickets:
Get them online at our website or at the Tourist Information in Bath.

Deine Familie möchte Bath besuchen. Du liest diesen Werbetext. Beantworte die Fragen deines Vaters.

Vater Diese Tour sieht sehr interessant aus. Wie lange dauert sie?

Du _____

Vater Ist das so eine Besichtigungstour, auf der man alles von einem Tonband erklärt bekommt? Das finde ich nämlich nicht so gut.

Du _____

Vater Das ist gut. Steht da, was man alles besichtigen kann?

Du _____

_____

Vater Kann man denn auch in den Zirkus gehen oder was soll das bedeuten?

Du _____

Vater Die englischen Parks gefallen mir gut. Kann man sich da auch aufhalten oder muss man immer bei der Gruppe bleiben?

Du _____

_____

Vater Jetzt noch zu den Preisen: Wir sind ja 2 Erwachsene und zwei Kinder.
Sara ist 6 und Peter, du bist 13. Was ist da am preiswertesten?

Du _____

_____

Vater Dann nehmen wir das mit dem Eintritt für die Roman Baths, denn die wollen wir ja unbedingt
besichtigen. Wo können wir die Tickets kaufen?

Du _____

SPEAKING

_____ / 15

🎧 16 **Learn English in Bath!**

*Today a reporter is visiting Bath Language School. She interviews some of the students there.
Listen to the interviewer's questions and José's answers.*

🎧 17 **Now you**

Now the reporter interviews Julian from Germany. Take his role.

*First listen to the reporter's questions again and then collect some ideas.
The information card about Julian can help you. Then answer the reporter's questions.*

☞
- Im Englischen klingt es eher unfreundlich, wenn man Fragen nur mit einem Wort beantwortet.
- Achte darauf, wo möglich, **short answers** (= Yes, it is. / No, it isn't. / Yes, I do. / No, I don't. Yes, I have. / No, I haven't) zu benutzen.
- Reichere deine Antworten mit echten Informationen an, um das Gespräch lebendiger zu machen.

Beispiel: Do you like Bath?
1 Yes. (klingt unfreundlich)
2 Yes, I do. Bath is a nice town. There are lots of interesting museums.
   And the Roman Baths are amazing. I went there yesterday. (klingt freundlicher)

BATH LANGUAGE SCHOOL   *Student information card*

Age: 16
Hometown: Leipzig
Information: • writes well but finds it difficult to speak English
             • thinks school is OK
             • has met new friends at school
             • is really happy with his host family[1] (one son / 16 years)
             • thinks Bath is a nice town
             • goes to too many discos!!!

[1] host family [haʊst]   *Gastfamilie*

Unit 6   Klassenarbeit B

Gesamtpunktzahl _____ / 55   Note _____

LISTENING

_____ / 11

 A birthday party at the Roman Baths

It's Sara's birthday. Her parents have booked a birthday party at the Roman Baths for Sara and her friends. Matthew from the Roman Baths has prepared the party for them. Listen to Matthew, Sara and Benny.

> **New word**
> Latin ['lætɪn] *lateinisch*

> 👉 Erinnere dich daran, dass du es leichter hast, wenn du dir vor dem Hören die Aufgaben genau durchliest. Dann weißt du, auf was du beim Hören achten musst.

1 Sara's Roman birthday

_____ / 3

Look at the pictures and write down the numbers of the pictures that you can hear something about in the text.

Numbers of the pictures:

2 All about the party

_____ / 8

Listen to the text again. Then tick (✔) the right box.

		Right	Wrong
1	They will go swimming.		
2	They will get something to eat and to drink at the Roman Baths.		
3	Sara and her friends will find out more about how the Romans lived.		
4	They can choose one activity.		
5	It's easy for Sara to choose the most interesting activity.		
6	Sara's friends want to look for things in the sand.		
7	Matthew teaches them some Latin words.		
8	At the end of the party every child has got a pair of Roman sandals.		

LANGUAGE   ____ / 27

1   WORDS Word building   ____ / 11

a) *Which words go together? Draw lines. Then write down the words that you found. (5P)*

Zusammensetzungen, bei denen die Wörter getrennt bleiben		Zusammensetzungen, bei denen die Wörter zusammengeschrieben werden	
post	store	care	pecker
police	centre	grand	ache
department	money	sweet	father
leisure	station	head	heart
pocket	office	wood	taker

1 _____   6 _____

2 _____   7 _____

3 _____   8 _____

4 _____   9 _____

5 _____   10 _____

b) *) Find the correct words. (6P)*

every   end   body   build

er   ment   week

play   inform   ing

ation   depart

1 _____   4 _____

2 _____   5 _____

3 _____   6 _____

2 WORDS Can you tell me the way?

_____ /7

Look at the map and explain the way.

☞	German	English
	Biegen Sie rechts in **die** Königstraße.	Turn right into ~~the~~ King Street.
	Im Deutschen setzen wir einen Artikel vor den Straßennamen.	Im Englischen folgt auf die Präposition direkt der Straßenname ohne Artikel.

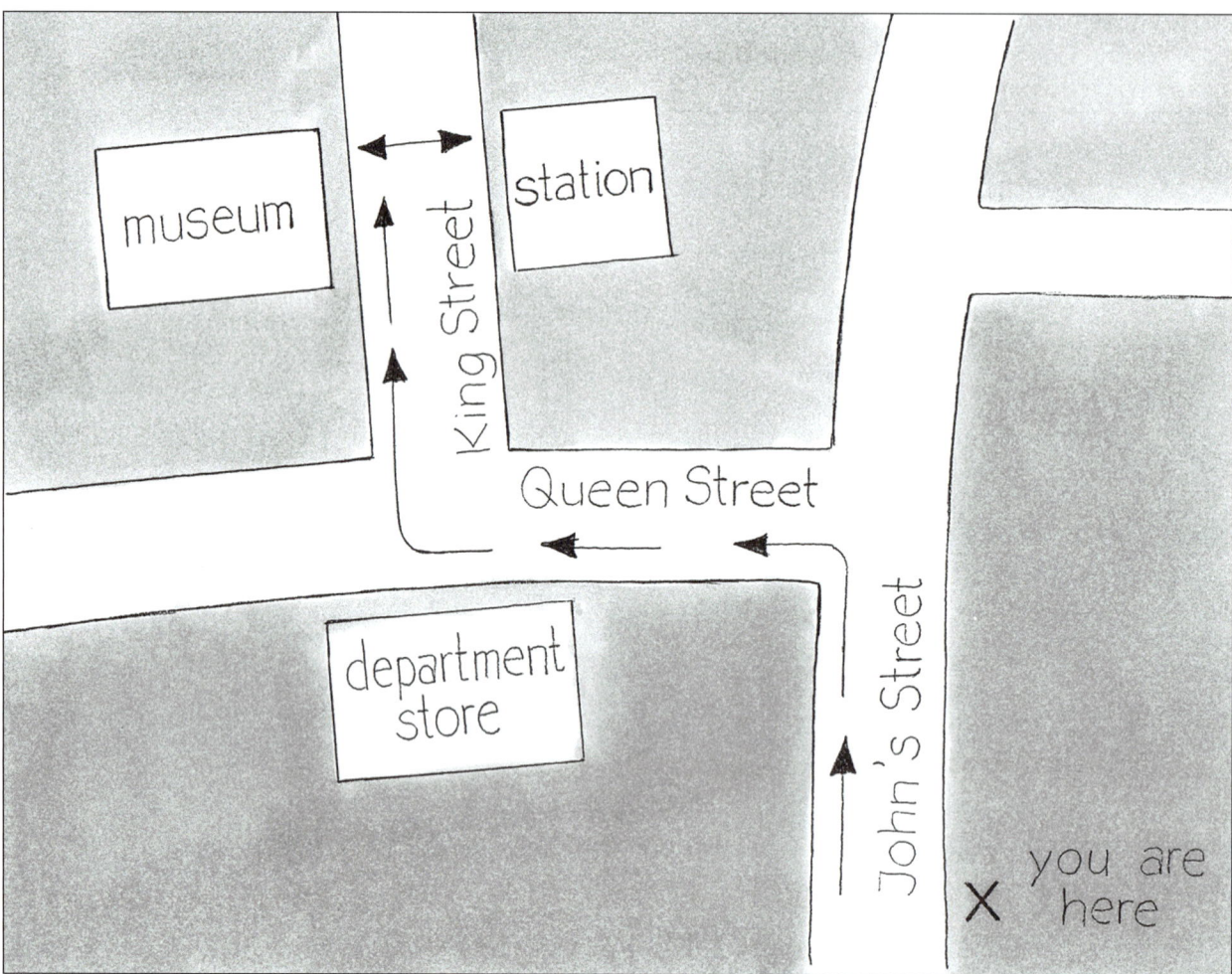

A tourist asks you the way from John's Street to the station. Write the dialogue:

Tourist Excuse me, _____.

You _____ John's Street. (1)

Then _____

_____

_____.

The station is _____.

Tourist _____.

3   STUDY SKILLS Correcting mistakes: Sara's invitation

_____ / 5

Sara has written invitation cards for her birthday. Correct the five spelling mistakes.
Cross out (✘) the wrong words and write down the text again with the right words. <u>Underline them</u>.

Dear Sue,
It's my birthday soon, so I'd like to invit you to my party.
It's a special party – a roman party.
The party will be on

5th July from 2 pm to 8 pm.

We'll meat at my house first and
than cycle to the museum together.

I hope you can come.
Let me no soon if you can come.

Love Sara

☞   Lies den Text langsam und aufmerksam, damit du die Rechtschreibfehler findest.
Achte auf:
– Vollständigkeit der Wörter: Sind alle Buchstaben da?
– Auf Groß- und Kleinschreibung: Was wird im Englischen großgeschrieben?
– Ist es das richtige Wort? Z. B. *see = sehen* oder *sea = Meer*?

_____

_____

_____

_____

_____

_____

_____

_____

_____

_____

_____

4 GRAMMAR When Sara's mum arrived

_____ / 4

Benny says what these people were doing when Sara's mum arrived at the Roman Baths birthday party.

When Sara's mum arrived ...

Pete _____.

I _____.

Sara _____.

Sophie and Lucy _____.

☞ Das **Past progressive** wird mit was/were + ing-Form gebildet.
Es wird oft benutzt, um auszudrücken, was gerade vor sich ging, als eine
zweite Handlung einsetzte: Jemand war gerade dabei etwas zu tun, als ...

WRITING

_____ / 17

Birthday party at the Roman Baths

Sue was one of Sara's guests. Look at the pictures and write a text for Sue's diary.
Say what you liked and what was funny. Use some of the linking words and adjectives in the box.

☞	Linking words	Adjectives
	at two o'clock • a few minutes • later • suddenly • then • next • so • but	funny • interesting • nice • great • amazing • beautiful • best • difficult • easy • exciting • fantastic • favourite • happy

1   meet – Sara's house

2   cycle to

3   man – tell plans for the afternoon

4   bring – Roman clothes put on – laugh

5   have – drinks, …

6   go round – look at

7   make sandals

8   cycle home

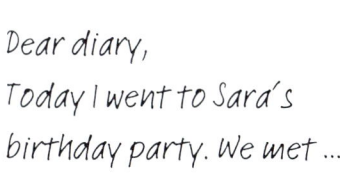

Dear diary,
Today I went to Sara's birthday party. We met …

☞ Wenn du im Tagebuch über **Vergangenes** berichtest, verwendest du das **Simple past**:
I talk**ed** to my friend …

Die volle Punktzahl bekommst du, wenn deine Lösung richtig ist und du die Arbeitsanweisung genau befolgt hast:
• Überprüfe, ob du geschrieben hast, was dir gefallen hat und was du lustig fandest.
• Überprüfe ob du **linking words** und **Adjektive** benutzt hast.

Kompetenztest

Im Laufe deines bisherigen Englischunterrichts hast du Hören, Lesen, Schreiben und Sprechen trainiert. Diese Kompetenzen benötigst du, um die englische Sprache zu beherrschen. Mithilfe dieses Kompetenztests kannst du einschätzen, welche dieser Fähigkeiten du schon kannst und welche du noch üben musst. An vielen Schulen werden in Klasse 6 Kompetenztests geschrieben. Sie werden auch Diagnosetests oder Vergleichsarbeiten genannt. Hier kannst du dich auf die Testsituation vorbereiten. Du hast 60 Minuten Zeit.

> Gesamtpunktzahl _____ / 80   Note _____

TEIL 1: LISTENING

_____ / 20

🎧 19 **AT A PARK IN PARIS**

There is an international skateboard contest in a park in Paris. Lily and Philip are watching. They meet Charlie. Listen to Charlie, Lily and Philip.

1 Countries and places

_____ / 4

Listen for the names of these countries or cities and tick (✔) them if you hear them.
*You must tick **four** boxes.*

1	Chester		6	Dover	
2	Gloucester		7	England	
3	Berlin		8	Germany	
4	Paris		9	London	
5	Belgium		10	France	

2 Charlie and Philip

_____ / 8

Listen again. What is correct about Charlie and Philip?
Decide if the sentence is right for Charlie or for Philip. You must tick (✔) eight boxes.

		Charlie	Philip
1	He is Lily's twin brother.		
2	He is from Dover.		
3	He is from Chester.		
4	His new school is great.		
5	He is on holiday in Paris.		
6	He lives in Paris.		
7	He came to Paris on Tuesday.		
8	He is with his uncle George.		

3   All about Lily and Philip's parents

_____ / 8

Listen again. Are these sentences right or wrong? Tick (✔) the right box.

		Right	Wrong
1	Their mum and dad are French.		
2	Their parents live in a park.		
3	Their mum likes Paris.		
4	Their dad has a job in Paris.		
5	Their dad worked in Dover.		
6	Their dad didn't like his job in Chester.		
7	Their dad loved English food.		
8	Their dad likes Paris.		

TEIL 2: SPEAKING

_____ / 20

1   At lunch break

_____ / 8

What can you see in this photo?

Where are these students?

What time of the day is it?

Why are they together?

What have they got on the table?

What are they doing?

🎧 20 **2   Your first day at a new school**   ____ / 12

You and your family have moved to another city. Today is your first day at the new school.
Your English teacher asks you some questions.

Teacher	Welcome to our school. Today is your first day, isn't it? It's good to have you here. How are you?
You	…
Teacher	What's your name?
You	…
Teacher	How old are you?
You	…
Teacher	Where are you from?
You	…
Teacher	Tell us something about your old school: the teachers, the students and your favourite subjects …
You	…
Teacher	Have you got brothers or sisters?
You	…
Teacher	What do you do in your free time?
You	…
Teacher	Tell us something about your last holiday: what was it like, where did you go and what did you do?
You	…
Teacher	That sounds interesting. Well, I'm sure you'll like it here at our school. The students here are really nice. So, all the best. Have a great first day!

TEIL 3: READING

_____ / 20

Gwen's holiday diary

Saturday

It was grey and cold when we started from Chester this morning. There was a lot of traffic, so it took us a long time to get to Kendal and we had to stop three times on the way because of Benny. He is nine, but he is a big baby. When we arrived in Kendal, it was too late for most things, so we went to _Kendal Leisure Centre_. It closes at eleven pm. Dad went to the sauna. Mum played with Benny in the baby pool. (Why can't he play with other kids?) I swam and I did the 50 metres in only a minute. Then we had fish and chips and ice cream. Benny didn't like his ice cream, so I had two.

Our bed & breakfast place is OK. The bad thing is that Benny and I have to be in one room together. I want to read my book but Benny says he can't sleep because of the lamp. Why can't he just shut his eyes?

Sunday

It was a wet Sunday. No sun. But it wasn't a problem. _Lakeland Climbing Centre_ is not outside. It's the biggest rock-climbing centre in the north of England and home to 'Kendal Wall', a great wall to climb. I made it all the way up!

In the afternoon the sun was out. Mum wanted to see the _Topiary Gardens_. It was boring – only old trees, but we had tea there at the Tea Room. Benny had hot chocolate, but he didn't drink it all, so I had tea and hot chocolate.

1 On the way to Kendal

_____ / 4

Tick (✔) the right ending. More than one ending can be correct for the numbers 1–3.
You must tick 4 endings.

1	When they started it was	a) morning.	
		b) afternoon.	
		c) evening.	
		d) Saturday.	
		e) Sunday.	
		f) nice.	

2	On the way to Kendal	a) they went very fast.	
		b) they had tea.	
		c) there was an accident.	
		d) they needed lots of time.	

3	When they arrived in Kendal	a) it was eleven in the morning.	
		b) it was eleven in the evening.	
		c) it was late.	
		d) everybody had ice cream.	

2   In Kendal on Saturday

_____/ 6

Tick (✔) the right box.

	Right	Wrong	Not in the text
1 They all went swimming at *Kendal Leisure Centre*.	☐	☐	☐
2 At *Kendal Leisure Centre* Gwen's mother bought Benny something to drink.	☐	☐	☐
3 Gwen's brother Benny is still a baby. He is nine months old.	☐	☐	☐
4 *Kendal Leisure Centre* is open late.	☐	☐	☐
5 Benny can't swim.	☐	☐	☐
6 Gwen is not happy because Benny and she have to sleep in the same room.	☐	☐	☐

3   In Kendal on Sunday

_____/ 7

Tick (✔) the right box.

	Right	Wrong	Not in the text
1 Sunday morning was nice.	☐	☐	☐
2 *Lakeland Climbing Centre* has no roof.	☐	☐	☐
3 It's the biggest climbing centre in England.	☐	☐	☐
4 *Kendal Wall* is 20 metres high.	☐	☐	☐
5 The *Topiary Gardens* are near the *Kendal Wall*.	☐	☐	☐
6 You can have a tea at the *Topiary Gardens*.	☐	☐	☐
7 Gwen drank hot chocolate there.	☐	☐	☐

4   Gwen

_____/ 3

Tick (✔) the right ending.

1 Gwen has got a brother. He's nine	a) and she likes playing with him.	☐
	b) and he doesn't like long trips in the car.	☐

2 On Saturday evening Gwen is angry because	a) Benny won't let her read.	☐
	b) Benny is talking to her.	☐

3 Gwen likes	a) climbing.	☐
	b) walking round parks and gardens.	☐

TEIL 4: WORDS AND WRITING

_____ / 20

1 WORDS A trip to Wales

_____ / 8

Complete the mind map.

```
              deer
         ┌──────────────┐
         │              │                      museum
  ┌───────────┐  ┌───────────┐          ┌──────────────┐
  │           │  │           │          │              │
  │_____│  │_____│   ┌───────────┐  ┌───────────┐
┌─────────────┐ ┌─────────────┐  │           │  │           │
│             │ │             │  │_____│  │_____│
│_____│ │_____│
```

animals   go sightseeing

what you can see on a trip   A trip to Wales   what you can do on a trip
to the countryside   to a town

nature   spend leisure time

```
  ┌───────────┐  ┌───────────┐          ┌───────────┐  ┌───────────┐
  │           │  │           │          │           │  │           │
  │_____│  │_____│          │           │  │           │
┌─────────────┐ ┌─────────────┐         │_____│  │_____│
│  mountains  │ │             │
│_____│ │_____│              ┌──────────────┐
                                             │  go shopping │
```

what it is like

in the countryside   in a town

```
  ┌───────────┐  ┌───────────┐                    ┌───────────┐  ┌───────────┐
  │   quiet   │  │           │                    │   dirty   │  │           │
  │_____│  │_____│                    │_____│  │_____│
┌─────────────┐                                  ┌─────────────┐
│_____│                                  │_____│
```

2   WRITING An e-mail about your last holiday

_____ / 12

Write an e-mail to your penfriend Steve about your last holiday.

Write a beginning and an ending. *Tell him:* • when you went (1P) • where you went (1P) • who went with you (1P) • where you stayed (1P) • what you did (2P) • what you liked about it (2P) • what you didn't like about it (2P)	*Use 'little' words from the list to make your sentences.* • and • so • but • too • also

_____

_____

_____

_____

_____

_____

_____